Life Begins with Jesus

by

George W. Wiseman

First Fruits Press
Wilmore, Kentucky
c2012

ISBN: 9781621710318

Life Begins with Jesus, by George W. Wiseman
First Fruits Press, © 2012
Previously published: Newton Centre: Mass. : the Modern Press, c1942.

Digital version at http://place.asburyseminary.edu/firstfruitsbooks/4/

First Fruits Press is a digital imprint of the Asbury Theological Seminary, B.L. Fisher Library. Asbury Theological Seminary is the legal owner of the material previously published by the Pentecostal Publishing Co. and reserves the right to release new editions of this material as well as new material produced by Asbury Theological Seminary. Its publications are available for noncommercial and educational uses, such as research, teaching and private study. First Fruits Press has licensed the digital version of this work under the Creative Commons Attribution Noncommercial 3.0 United States License. To view a copy of this license, visit http://creativecommons.org/licenses/by-nc/3.0/us/.

For all other uses, contact:

First Fruits Press
B.L. Fisher Library
Asbury Theological Seminary
204 N. Lexington Ave.
Wilmore, KY 40390
http://place.asburyseminary.edu/firstfruits

Wiseman, George W.
   Life begins with Jesus / by George W. Wiseman.
   Wilmore, Ky. : First Fruits Press, c2012.
   189 p. ; 21 cm.
   Reprint. Previously published: Newton Centre: Modern Press, c1942.
   ISBN: 9781621710318 (pbk.)
   1. Sermons, American. I. Title.
BV4253 .W755 2012

Cover design by David Roux

LIFE BEGINS WITH JESUS

Copyright, 1942, by
GEORGE W WISEMAN
First Printing — September, 1942

THE MODERN PRESS
NEWTON CENTRE, MASS.
Printed in U. S. A.

LIFE BEGINS WITH JESUS

By
GEORGE W. WISEMAN
Author of "LIFE BEGINS WITH FAITH"

THE MODERN PRESS
NEWTON CENTRE   MASSACHUSETTS

PREFACE

These are the first sermons preached following the death of a loved one and reveal the direction in which one, burdened by sorrow, faces. Many of the intimate references and poems that appear throughout the book, although in the original manuscript, were not used. This, I am sure, can be readily understood. Not a reassuring word or reference to life everlasting, however, were omitted, for at no time is one called upon to demonstrate his faith or prove what he has preached to be sufficient for life's crisis hours, than when this experience, common to all, comes to his own home.

The sermons are not arranged in the order of their delivery. "Conquerors, Plus" was the first prepared. That so many were inspired by the Gospel of John is not accidental, for from its chapters satisfying assurance and genuine comfort were received.

My prayer, as I send forth this volume, is that the sorrowful might find comfort, faith be reborn, and love and devotion to the Master be increased through the reading of these pages.

George W Wiseman

To
the memory of
ELSIE MARGARET WISEMAN
whose devotion
and loving ministry
was a constant reminder
of the Master.

TABLE OF CONTENTS

Christ's Most Amazing Statement	9
Impressive Boldness	23
Life Begins With Jesus	35
What We Need Most	49
Conquerors, Plus	61
What Christ Would Do For Us	75
Why Leave Jesus?	87
A Peep Into Heaven	99
Paul's Cleverest Saying	111
What Should We Learn From Jesus?	123
The World's Greatest Need	137
The Master's Spirit Of Thanksgiving	149
The Peace Christ Gives	161
Out-Lived Sorrow	175

CHRIST'S MOST AMAZING STATEMENT

"In the world ye shall have tribulation: but be of good cheer; I have overcome the world." — JOHN 16:33

THE MOST unusual and challenging words ever uttered came from the lips of Jesus. The world has never ceased to marvel at them. He made greater claims for Himself than did anyone else. And He did it with such assurance that even His most skeptical listeners wondered. Coming from His lips the impossible seemed possible. The greatest mysteries appeared common.

As we read we also become aware of His matter-of-fact tone. He never shouted in an endeavor to impress upon others something they might consider untrue. He never hurried or made an attempt to justify His statements. He was not afraid of unfriendly questions. He had an answer for all. He spoke the truth and backed His words with His life. As unreal as His message sounded to others ears, His sincerity and bearing indicated how natural it appeared to Him. He never apologized for what He said. It was not given in haste or under tension. Neither was it due to a slip of the tongue or error in judgment. Every day of His short ministry He startled His listeners. "Never man spake like this man," was more than an expression of awe.

Perhaps the most arresting claims were given in the upper room with only His disciples present. Even the men who had walked with Him from the day He first called them questioned Him on this occasion. They had grown accustomed to His electrifying words and expected most anything. Yet the message of that night caused them to ask for explanations and enlargements. His most amazing statement was given previous to their departure for Gethsemane, when He said, "Be of good cheer; I have overcome the world." Perhaps the disciples were too mystified by this time to reply. They understood the situation as well as did Jesus. Opposition had reached such a peak that something would happen soon. This they knew. The world He claimed to have overcome was crying for His blood. Never had there been such a night. Storms of anger and cries for vengeance raged without. Yet in the quiet of the upper room the Master calmly said, "Be of good cheer," and then added, "I have overcome the world."

This verse contains so much that is needed for the present hour of the world's confusion, that we cannot view the last words without giving attention to the first. In the first place, Jesus prepared His disciples for the future by indicating their place of refuge. The assurance of peace is tremendously important. If the Master did not possess it, He could not have finished this chapter as He did. Surely He would not have been able to meet the onslaught of the world with the same courageous spirit He did a few hours later. The serenity He possessed in the upper room continued to the end. And that which faced Him He knew would also greet His disciples. They must be prepared. It would be impossible to face the future without this inner peace. It was essential. He had alluded to it several times that evening. It was important that they understand its necessity. "These things have I spoken unto you." He was not wasting words. They were spoken for a purpose. They must believe them, as intensely

CHRIST'S MOST AMAZING STATEMENT

as He did. "That in me ye might have peace." That peace was to come from Him, not the world.

In the parable of the vine and branches He said, "Abide in me," and now only a short time later, He reminded them again that peace would come only by abiding in Him. He held the key to their future. If they deserted Him they would meet only defeat. But more than that, they would forsake the peace that belonged to them. We notice later, when they did desert momentarily, it was peace they sacrificed. Unable to find peace, Peter decided to return to his old life of fishing. It was to be a temporary trip, to be sure, but it indicates the absence of peace. The disciples because of fear huddled together in the safety of the upper room with doors securely locked. Thomas was so troubled in mind that he refused to meet with them. Jesus foresaw this and indirectly warned them of the disastrous results to their peace if they failed to abide in Him.

If we haven't already gone through the same dilemma experienced by the disciples, we will unless we possess the Master's peace and abide in Him. "I am at peace with all men and God is at peace with me," Richard Hooker triumphantly exclaimed on the eve of his departure for that Eternal Home in 1600, "and from this blessed assurance I feel that inward joy which the world can neither give or take away." This assurance is gained only through intimate fellowship with Christ.

The world is a master at disturbing peace. Life has a way of breaking happy bonds and troubling human minds. In that hour strong men cry aloud, "There is no peace," and weak men crumble before the onslaught for which they were unprepared. The tragedy is only emphasized the more when we realize that the destruction of peace comes at the time when we thought it to be most secure. It is hard to realize that the sun which has always been friendly and warm would suddenly disappear in the face of an icy blast that has apparently descended from nowhere. Life is like that. Peace and security are guaranteed no one.

"The man who has found God has not insured himself against calamity," says Leslie D. Weatherhead, "but he has found One who will show him how to turn calamity into triumph." Indeed he has! That is what Jesus was trying to say, but it is disquieting to know that hardships must be faced. This was the shock that came to the disciples when they left the friendly, peaceful atmosphere of the upper room. How unbelievable that Jesus would be arrested and later crucified! Peter immediately took his sword. Jesus was his security. They were at peace when they were with Him. To have Him arrested was to remove that from their lives. Yet arrested He was, and with it came the icy blasts. They were alone, facing the same men He faced, the same unfriendly world He had warned against. But their experience is common to all who have not learned the lesson He tried so hard to teach. We cannot ridicule them without accusing ourselves. Jesus knows what is before us tomorrow as well as He did that which faced His own disciples, and His message is the same: "These things I have spoken unto you, that in me ye might have peace."

In the second place, Jesus revealed what loomed before them. "In the world ye shall have tribulation." There it is! He has opened the windows. They can see for themselves. It begins tomorrow. That is what makes the sentence before us so meaningful. We must, of course, bear in mind that the world they looked upon was different from that which we view. They were surrounded by men and nations that knew nothing of the God proclaimed by Jesus. The spirit of Christ had not penetrated. It was a world so completely hostile that the disciples' tribulations would assume the character of persecution and death. However, the fact that our world is considered Christian doesn't undermine the strength and importance of these words. When applied to certain sections of Europe, at the present moment, they are as meaningful as when Jesus first uttered them. Neither are they weakened when applied to us.

Not only is our world antagonistic to much Jesus said, but tribulation indicates pressure, and pressure is an experience common to all. Often it is an inner pressure. One thing is sure, the more we try to live like the Master the greater the pressure or tribulation. Take the matter of temptation. The person removed from Jesus doesn't allow it to bother him. He doesn't fight against it, nor the world find cause to use force. But place the Christian in the same surroundings and it takes a different course. This principle applies to every hard or trying situation in which we are placed.

Sometimes the pressure comes from without. The disciples faced tribulation because they followed Jesus. Those who listened to the Master but did not respond to His invitation were not molested. They could safely stand at the foot of the cross, or be on the edge of the multitude bent upon the destruction of His followers, yet go their way unharmed. Those whom we feel should be divinely led and protected face the greatest pressure. But this is no reason for us to lose faith. Jesus never said that a smooth road would stretch before His disciples. His appeal was to hardship, not ease. "Take up the cross and follow me. In the world ye shall have tribulation." It would almost seem that if life is unusually easy for us, there is something wrong with our discipleship. If life is difficult let us not be frightened. Let us not turn back and walk with Him no more. Rather may we remember that this is what He said would happen.

Thomas Lee and his wife played a decisive role in the establishment of Methodism. He was stoned, dragged roughly down stairs, sustaining an injury to his back from which he never fully recovered, rolled in a sewer, and finally thrown in a river. His wife, who came to his aid, was struck in the mouth till it bled. While preaching at Pately his head was broken with a stone. Yet he said of that experience, "It was a glorious time and several date their conversion from that day." That is what Jesus knew would happen to his disciples. If they could shout, "It was a glorious time, conversions resulted churches were born," would it not be worth it? This is a far cry from the little puttering we do and fondly call it Christianity. The tinkering that consumes so much of our time. We are always busy, but with the outward pressure relaxed our accomplishments for the Master are not equal to our hot endeavors.

CHRIST'S MOST AMAZING STATEMENT

Perhaps the hardest thing for us to realize is that tribulations are beneficial. There are many unwelcome intrusions that we cry bitterly against. Jesus was not cruel when He said, "In the world ye shall have tribulation." Yet He was not only stating a fact, but knew this was what His disciples needed to bring out that which they had not yet shown.

Tribulation is the greatest revealer of what a person is. We will never know, and neither will others, what is really inside of us until we are sorely tried. We might revel in our strength, but that hour may reveal our weakness. On the other hand, we might gain a strength that we never knew existed. "No one knows," said Borden Parker Bowne, "what it is to walk with God in the deepest sense who has not walked with Him in the dark." The darkest hour vividly outlines the Eternal.

But tribulation does more than reveal. Whenever we meet genuine, sympathetic, understanding individuals we find that in almost every case they are the ones who have come out of great tribulation. They have experienced life's worst, yet have not grown bitter. Barrie, in *Margaret Oglivy,* has a chapter on, "How My Mother Got Her Soft Face." Her boy, away from home, received a serious injury. She immediately made plans to hasten to his bedside where she might minister to him. The tickets were bought and the farewells had been said, when a telegram arrived saying he was gone. The shock was tremendous and the broken-hearted mother never fully recovered. But it made her a finer, gentler woman. "That," says Barrie, "is how my mother got her soft face and her pathetic ways and her large charity, and why mothers run to her when they have lost a child." The cost is great to the one acquiring a soft face and a sympathetic understanding, sufficient to draw the sorrowful, relieve their distress, and return them to their homes comforted. Whenever God desires to make a strong, beautiful life, He places that life in some crossroads of pain.

> I walked a mile with Pleasure,
>   She chattered all the way;
> But left me none the wiser
>   For all she had to say.
>
> I walked a mile with Sorrow,
>   And ne'er a word said she;
> But, oh, the things I learned from her
>   When Sorrow walked with me.

If you wish to learn of the goodness of God, or the assurance of life everlasting, seek it from the lips of one who has spent long hours in some dark Gethsemane. Tribulation is beneficial, yet we do not yearn for it. We do not desire to grow by that method. If we had our way it would be unknown. I imagine that is why God made life as He did. We might question His wisdom and argue that life is unfair, but He knew what was best for our welfare, so He placed tribulation in the center and made it the beating heart of onward progress.

Another difficulty is to harmonize tribulation with peace. When tribulation comes peace seems to take wings. Peace is always the mark of a happy home. But it has been present because all has gone well. The

CHRIST'S MOST AMAZING STATEMENT

family has been healthy. Money has come in regularly. Worries have been at a minimum. Then suddenly something unwanted, perhaps never dreamed of, has happened. It might be a very serious illness that eventually terminated in death. The end came after months of hope, when we were almost sure our loved one would live. When that happens, we immediately feel peace has been destroyed. Harmony, happiness, and a joy that has been bubbling over, seem suddenly to have ended.

If this should be your experience at this moment, then it is to you I address these words. Peace need not be lost. It can be restored. Your loved one cannot be replaced, but a peace deeper than any that has yet been experienced can come to you. Up until this point peace has been of a surface variety. This cannot always last and is the easiest to be broken. That doesn't mean your life has been lived away from God. You might have been a sincere disciple but it takes shadows to deepen and make vital even the things of the spirit.

If you are a mother, you will remember what made the difference between womanhood and motherhood. Mothers are made only by going through the valley and shadow that precedes the birth of the baby. It is that that gives birth to a mother's love. The world can never take that away. It is the valley and shadow that places the lustre on a mother's face and lights it with a smile that has never before appeared. Peace is born the same way. It comes not by dwelling on what has taken place but by dwelling in the Peace Giver. It was so natural for Jesus to have peace in the midst of tribulation that we hardly stop to ask the reason. Yet the reason is clear. It was because His life was one with His Father. That is why He could use peace and tribulation in one sentence and add to it the note of courage and joy, "Be of good cheer."

The third thing Jesus did was to place a light in the midst of darkness. After pointing out the pathway before them, He sought to bring them courage. These disciples needed words of encouragement. That evening He had stressed three things. The first, that He was going to leave them. He wanted to make this unmistakably clear. That thought would fail to arouse their enthusiasm. The second was a reminder of their weakness. They felt equal to any emergency. Sheltered by Him as they were during the past few years, they gave little thought to danger. Especially was that true with the greatest danger of all — weakness within. Jesus wanted them to know the truth. He pointed out the betrayer, and warned Peter that he would deny Him. The third thing He did was an attempt to make them understand that they must continue where He left off. That was not easy. The disciples always appeared slow in realizing what Jesus meant and now He had told them that to carry on His work would mean persecution. Tribulation could not be escaped. It was not a happy outlook. Yet in the midst of this darkness He held before them a light. He had done that all evening, when He spoke of His "Father's house," when He said, "Peace I leave with you, I will not leave you comfortless, I am the way, the truth, and the life." These were lighted windows of hope and encouragement. Now He had just said, "Be of good cheer."

CHRIST'S MOST AMAZING STATEMENT

This was a call to courage. Not the courage of the Stoic, which was the courage stressed by paganism. Many still feel that Stoicism is the only way out of sorrow. They grit their teeth, refuse to shed a tear, attempt to bear the heaviest burden by way of their own strength. In so doing their nerves become snarled and knotted. There is apt to be a breakdown. This is not the Master's way out of a hard situation. The courage to which He referred came from absolute trust in God. It depended upon an inner peace, not an inner tension. It was not bravado placed on from without, but a banishment of fear that took place within.

When we take Christ at His word fears will disappear. We will shed tears. We will mourn those whom we have lost awhile. Love is the most natural thing in life, and love grows, not diminishes when dear ones leave us. Jesus wept. He faced the cross by way of a prayer of agony. But He had a courage within that knew no fear and it is this He held before His disciples. He was the greatest reason for their lack of fear. He would be with them and we can be sure He still stands between us and tribulation. That is the foundation of courage. That is the source of being of good cheer.

The fourth thing Jesus did was to give the reason for this courage. "I have overcome the world." What an amazing statement! Especially in view of the picture that comes to us from the upper room where the shadow of the cross is so clearly discernible. Because of that reflection would you not say that the world was about to overcome Him? But let us not forget the at-homeness of Jesus. He was at home with God. The world had sought to destroy that fellowship but had not succeeded. He had overcome in that respect. He was at home with every plan God had for righteousness; every hope for distressed, sinful humanity; every heart pain for the suffering and sorrow of His own.

Shortly before my wife passed away, I asked her if she was still praying. We never knew her inner thoughts. Not once did she complain of her suffering. There were many things I wanted to know from the moment the doctor said there was little hope, but I withheld my questions for fear she would become aware of the seriousness of her illness. During the last few days there was a question whether or not she could concentrate on one thought long enough to carry it through to completion. However, her answer dispelled any doubts I might have had. "I'm praying all the time," came her weak reply. I knew these prayers were not all for herself, for I knew her. In her suffering she became increasingly conscious of the goodness of God. She was with Him long before He whispered, "Come." It was this at-homeness Jesus had with His Father and which He was anxious that His disciples share. He had overcome in that direction. The world had failed in its attempt to overcome Him.

"But the cross," we cry, "what about that?" Well what about it? Wasn't that but another step in His program of overcoming? His enemies did not gain a victory by way of the crucifixion. The victory was His. His conquest not only centered around His day but extended down the long avenues of the future. That was

CHRIST'S MOST AMAZING STATEMENT

definitely settled at Calvary. It came at the moment heads wagged and men headlined His defeat. He overcame death and in so doing opened before mankind doors leading into a richer, fuller life. Jesus conquered in every realm that mattered.

This means that every Christian now has a shelter. Today the word "shelter" is being heavily underlined. It has always been synonymous with life, but life for a few. It now includes entire nations. When wan faces, searching the sky, sight off in the distance dread black specks that are hardly discernible, or when sirens sound, old men and women, mothers with nursing babes in their arms, little children and all others not assigned to important defense positions, rush to their air raid shelters. It is their haven of refuge.

In this world Christ is the shelter to which we can go. Men might still kill their fellowmen, lawlessness prevail, and Jesus be exposed to ridicule and scorn, but He conquered in the realm of the spiritual and that is where the Christian should live. What if men do seek to destroy the body or heap contempt upon us because of our faith? With Jesus, we live above that, and we can become conquerors too, for we have a shelter in Him. "Fear not them which kill the body, but are not able to kill the soul," He once said to His disciples. That is the secret of an unruffled spirit, calm assurance and an unshaken faith. In the midst of this world's conflict I penned the poem, "Be Calm, My Soul."

> Be calm, my soul, though faced with endless sorrow,
> Wrought by unrighteous men whose souls have flown;
> For God will have His turn with them tomorrow,
> When they must face Him, naked and alone.

LIFE BEGINS WITH JESUS

Be calm, my soul, amidst the world's confusion,
Produced by man — all else obeys His will;
Fear not the mass who welcome sin's intrusion,
They too shall pass, then oh, my soul, be still.

Be calm, my soul, life's hourglass unfailing,
Reveals the coming doom of armored might;
His Kingdom only waits the great unveiling,
The present darkness but obscures its light.

Be calm, my soul, but rise with faith, persistent,
To break the chains of doubt, distrust and greed;
Be calm, but yet inspire a zeal consistent,
To work with Him until mankind is freed.

"Who are these that are arrayed in white robes and whence came they?" Why, don't you know? "These are they which came out of great tribulation, and have washed their robes, and have made them white in the blood of the Lamb." They have found Christ their shelter amidst great tribulation here and find Him their place of refuge there. "Therefore are they before the throne of God, and serve Him day and night in His temple." Because Jesus overcame the world He made it possible for every follower to do likewise. He is our refuge both now and forever.

IMPRESSIVE BOLDNESS

"When they saw the boldness of Peter and John, . they took knowledge of them, that they had been with Jesus."
—Acts 4:13

EVERY MAN is a potential hero. All he needs is a great cause or a ruthless persecution to bring to the surface that which has long remained dormant. There were no cowards on Bataan or Corregidor, yet a few years ago many of these gallant defenders were our neighbors, living quiet, unpretentious lives.

Every Christian has within him the making of a Niemoeller or a Kagawa. Whenever we desire proof of what Christianity can do for one when it is taken with all seriousness, let us read the book of Acts. Christ has a way of gripping men, shaking them from indifference, and sending them forth to save a world, regardless of personal danger. The disciples were ordinary men, possessing little outward power before Pentecost. Jesus had spent many discouraging hours attempting to train them, but that was now a matter of the past. Our text is an illustration of the change that had been wrought.

Peter and John had healed a lame man at the gate of the Temple. The unusual miracle was sufficient to gather a crowd, and the disciples, ever looking for an opportunity, preached unto them Jesus and the resurrection. Although the multitude seemed eager to listen to the words of Peter, the rulers were alarmed. Not long before they had crucified Jesus, certain that that was the end. However, they had learned recently that His followers were appearing everywhere and the boldest were in their midst, already having made thousands of converts. This had to be stopped, so the arrest of Peter and John was ordered.

It is recorded that Lord Melbourne, the first Prime Minister of Queen Victoria, angerly retorted after listening to a pointed sermon, "Religion is all very well but it's getting a bit too far when it claims to interfere with a man's private life." Not only were the rulers incensed over the daring of the Apostles, but like their Master they were interfering with the accepted standards in government, business and private life.

The next morning, after a night in prison, they were brought before the council. To their amazement the rulers found that imprisonment had not dampened the ardor of the two before them. Instead, Peter began preaching, insisting that salvation was impossible apart from Christ. The council had difficulty determining what course should be followed. Imprisonment was not the answer. It was impossible to keep them confined longer, especially with a healed man in their midst who had been lame from birth. And they had a healthy respect for their courage, for "when they saw the boldness of Peter and John, they took knowledge of them, that they had been with Jesus." So with a warning not to continue their preaching they let them go.

"The boldness of Peter!" These are strange words, are they not? So unlike the picture presented by the Gospels. It is true that he is not always portrayed as a coward, but his courage flared when surrounded by strong men. He did not, however, possess the courage that would enable him to stand, unyielding, when alone.

IMPRESSIVE BOLDNESS

When Jesus called him he resembled soft, easily moving sand. It was the Master who gave him the name suggesting a rock. He had not attained that rock foundation, but the faith of Jesus was not in what he was but what he could become. Three years passed, yet courage did not characterize his life. Nervously he warmed himself over a fire in the courtyard, vehemently denying his discipleship when accused by a girl servant. Yet that which the rulers noticed on this occasion was not cowardice but boldness. He was a different Peter. Something had happened.

They also noticed the boldness of John. He was steady and reliable, apparently liked by friend and foe, but would never be associated with courage. It was he who leaned his head on his Master's bosom. Love was always the keynote of his teaching. John was neither effeminate nor a weakling. He merely possessed a desire to keep out of trouble. At the beginning of his ministry he did want the Master to call fire from heaven to destroy a group who were hostile, but that was the result of anger, for which this fine, conscientious young man was always sorry. He stood at the foot of the cross with the weeping women, the only disciple to do so, but that was because he was so well known and accepted, rather than courage. But now, as in the case of Peter, it was his boldness that was recognized by the council. Something had likewise happened to John.

It is this that will happen to us if we take Jesus seriously. Yes, reminds the New Testament, that courage can come to every man, woman and young person

LIFE BEGINS WITH JESUS

who dare follow Christ. There is no mystery about it. The difference between the ordinary, routine Christian and the daring disciple possessing brave assurance, rests in the degree to which he accepts, believes and follows Jesus.

In the first place, a boldness that is impressive is impossible apart from assurance. The council realized how useless it was to warn Peter and John against preaching Christ. They were so sure of what they believed that not even the prospects of death would stop them. This is the assurance the Master expects us to possess.

It is relatively easy at times to allow the experiences of life to tame and subdue us—we who once stood bravely before the world willing to accept whatever was in store for us. With great faith in God we faced life unafraid, and we meant it. We were sincere. We knew in whom we believed and were persuaded that He was able to keep us. It was the glorious vision of youth that had yet to face the crushing, staggering blows of life. But how is it now? Are we still as courageous, still as sure? We ought to be, claims Jesus, and hastens to open to our view the book of Acts that we might see the boldness of His first disciples, who were no longer living a sheltered life with Him, but were out facing crosses, dungeons and arenas. This should be our experience. The courageous attitude of youth should grow with difficulties, not diminish. We were meant, by God's help, to tame and subdue life in order that it might fit into His plans. If we are as sure of Jesus as the Apostles were, we will still be in the front lines,

IMPRESSIVE BOLDNESS

ever on the offensive. Crushing problems will come, but if they do not cause us to grow in faith, we will have failed to see the strongest hand God extends in our direction.

This assurance must mean more than the comfort it brings us. We must be certain that the Master can save the most impossible, hopeless-looking individuals in this world, and we must help Him do it. That was what Peter and John were doing. They were preaching to those who had crucified Him. They were back in the city that hustled Him to a cross. It was not a suburb they selected, where people were tolerant and respectable. They served them, too, but their interest centered around those who hated and despised the One whose name they bore. And in that they were but following His footsteps.

Are you not amazed as you read the Gospels at the faith Jesus had in the redemption of the outcasts of His day? Even the disciples were repulsed by the sinfulness of the woman drawing water at Sychar's well, and at that time they were only saints in the making. Yet to her Jesus offered the water of life, outwardly calm and unhurried in His ministry, certain that she would accept. Who else could have seen a glorious future for such a person? It was this spirit that Peter and John now possessed. They were as sure as their Master had been, that these people with hate in their hearts, sin deeply ingrained in their lives and blood upon their hands, could be saved. And that is what He says to us. "They can be saved," He says repeatedly. "These souls that seem unpromising, that appear too calloused to be touched, too hard to be moved, can be saved." And He points to the various nations that take apparent delight in inflicting punishment on helpless, conquered people, and reminds us, "I mean them. They, too, can be saved."

In the second place, a boldness that is impressive signifies an awareness of power sufficient for every experience. The disciples were continually conscious of this power. Even when results seemed meagre in comparison to the sacrifice involved, they were not depressed. They could sing in prison as well as at an early morning service in a home attended by new converts. They expected something to happen, whether in Jerusalem or a more unpromising field of ministry, and they were not disappointed. Something did happen. That appears on every page in the book of Acts. Never once do we stumble upon the suggestion that they considered their labor to be in vain. Instead, they possessed a hope that they refused to let go. They were sure God would lead them and Christ would continue to empower them. That, they remind us, is what we need.

Are we aware of a sustaining power sufficient for every difficult experience of life? What would happen to our faith if our cherished plans should suddenly break around our feet? If the hand of tragedy should reach out and embrace us as it has vast multitudes in Europe and the Pacific? Would the world read our lives in terms of divine boldness? Would we demonstrate that we were certain there was a power stronger than that of fierce, unrelentless destruction? We are to be pitied if that faith is not ours as we face the furious, devastating assaults of the present hour, for no man can tell

IMPRESSIVE BOLDNESS

when it will turn in his direction. Peter and John did not relish pain or yearn for suffering. Their desire was to preach Christ and convert the unconverted. Yet pain and suffering came to them, but the record of their lives reveal they were equal to the most crushing blows. It is that that is expected of us.

If we believe this power possible, we will not only be anxious to work, but willing to perform the hardest tasks. Unfortunately, there prevails the thought that only ministers are called upon to do that which laymen did in the early church. Perhaps the church is to blame for this misunderstanding. A church official once said, "No wonder our churches are dying. Most ministers are no longer interested in saving souls. They would rather preach on topics of the day." I reminded him that our churches were not dying. Souls were being saved and for the most part ministers are the ones responsible. Then I suggested, that in view of his apparent concern and fervor, why did he not go out and save others? To which he replied. "I'm not getting paid for it, and you ministers are."

When we have caught the spirit and passion of Jesus we will save souls, regardless of the source from which our pay comes. This is one field upon which no group has a monopoly. When one who has slipped has been revived, or a soul drawn nearer the Kingdom, it matters not to Jesus whether it has been done through the efforts of a minister or consecrated layman. We are all disciples, and that which was uppermost upon His mind should be indelibly printed upon ours. "Get the tools ready," said Browning, "God will find thee work."

LIFE BEGINS WITH JESUS

I have in my possession a letter written very carefully, but indicating the unsteady hand of age. The writer belonged to the generation preceding this, and the words should bring a blush of shame to our faces. It reads as follows:

> Dear Pastor:
>
> If you are at a loss just to whom to assign your *very hardest prospects* for personal evangelism, and knowing my unfitness, you think that I am worthy to undertake such a task, I will gladly attempt to win them in Jesus' name.

It was signed only by the initials of the writer. Only a person with the spirit of Peter and John could write for an assignment to visit the very hardest prospects in an attempt to win them in Jesus' name. Have you written such a letter to your Pastor? Would you if the occasion demanded?

Finally, a courageous consecrated life is always a reminder of Jesus. When the council witnessed the boldness, fervor and determination of Peter and John "they took knowledge of them that they had been with Jesus." This is more than a mere recognition of the fact that they were followers of His. They had known that for years. Their names had been linked with Jesus from the beginning of His ministry, and their power had been spread abroad since His crucifixion. Rather do these words suggest that in them they could see the One who had stood in their midst not long before. It was His spirit they possessed, and that is the great message of the hour. It is not enough for others to hear that we are Christians. That which is essential is that they see

IMPRESSIVE BOLDNESS

in us the spirit of Christ, and as a result recognize that we have been with Him.

"That," we cry, "is impossible. We cannot possess the boldness of Peter and John in a world such as this. It would ruin our reputation and cause people to look upon us as queer." Others insist that they lack the necessary moral and spiritual strength to continue to live righteously, without attempting to minister. Jesus, however, has an answer for that. "I need you," He says, "even you who say it is impossible, for my kingdom cannot be built apart from you." He is aware of the peril and suffering it will cost. The New Testament nowhere leaves out the hard, but repeats over and over again that it is hardship, peril and suffering that make a man big, that give him boldness, increase the spirit of Christ and set him apart. If we had our way we would grow by some other means. Many of our prayers have been for the avoidance of the difficult, but as Jean Ingelow confessed, "I have lived to thank God that all my prayers have not been answered."

Jesus also insists that He can manage us. However weak and frail we are in body, no matter how faltering and unsteady we are spiritually, He can manage us. Never does He tire of us because of our failures. Neither does He leave us because we have sinned.

Think of the faith He had in those He met during His ministry! He once looked upon a man whose heart had become hardened, but He knew He could take care of Matthew and called him to be a disciple, and the first Gospel came from his pen. Mary Magdalene, a woman of the streets, was considered by the moral code of her day a fit subject for verbal and physical abuse, yet He touched her and had faith in her redemption. Later, she stood at the foot of the cross, broken-hearted, and was among the first to visit the tomb on Easter morning. And even the multitude, the unappreciative crowd that listened to His teachings, did not destroy His hope. "I can manage even them," He insisted, and went to the cross to prove that His faith in them was not misplaced or in vain. And Christ did manage them and He can manage us.

The other word He speaks is, "I can use you. I need you; I can manage you; I can use you." To Peter, still blushing with shame because of his denial, Jesus said, "I can use you. Feed my lambs, feed my sheep." And that is what Peter was doing when he was brought before the council. It is this same message He speaks to us, and we, poor souls, become ill at ease and confused, rapidly shifting from one foot to the other, complaining that He has made a mistake. However, a mistake hasn't been made. He knows that a change must take place, but He is equally sure that with us a transformation is possible.

Before books are published, galley proofs are printed upon which usually appear numerous mistakes. These are run down and corrected by carefully trained proof readers, who patiently remain at their task, seemingly unmindful of the labor involved. When the book is completed, the mistakes of the galley proofs are no longer in evidence. Instead, we hold in our hands a book worthy to be seen and read of men. "That," says Jesus, "is what your life is. You are galley proofs now,

IMPRESSIVE BOLDNESS

with glaring mistakes everywhere upon the surface. These mistakes must be corrected before you can be used, but working together we can do it. Then I can send you forth to be read by the world, not as uncorrected proofs, but as completed books." He knows what we can become. He realizes that when the corrections are made, the world looking upon us and reading our lives will take knowledge that we have been with Him.

LIFE BEGINS WITH JESUS
"I am the life." — JOHN 14:6

THE PURPOSE of Jesus' coming was to bestow life. "I am come that they might have life, and that they might have it more abundantly. I am the resurrection and the life; he that believeth on me, though he die, yet shall he live, and whosoever liveth and believeth on me shall never die. I am the way, the truth, and the life." These are tremendous claims. If all He did was to make them and they were never experienced by man, therefore no one was sure, what a cruel jest to play upon trusting, yearning humanity. It would make no difference how much He talked about changing man or the world; if His words were mere expressions or even sincere aspirations that could not be fulfilled, change would not take place. Life would remain the same. But this has not been the experience. Rather has it been that life begins with Jesus. "Indeed it does," exclaims the Apostle Paul. "It is no longer I that liveth, but Christ liveth in me." And that is life! It is always life when a man can shout triumphantly, "Christ lives in me," and men have done that from the moment of their first contact with Him.

He came to provide instructions concerning the life He was to give. To live is important, but how to live is more important. "I am the life," He said, "learn of me." And He taught men how to live by His life as well as His words. The way to possess life is to accept Him, affirms the New Testament, and continue with Him in an unbroken fellowship. "Ye will not come unto me that ye might have life," are among the most tragic words uttered. There were many who entreated Him to leave when He came into their midst. The citizens of Gerasa begged Him to depart from their coasts after sanity had been restored to one of their own, the result of His love, understanding, and power. They considered swine to be of greater value than the Life Giver and the person to whom life had been given.

The more we live with Jesus the more like Him we become. Martin Luther once said, "If you knock at my breast and ask, 'Who lives here? Luther?' my answer is, 'No! Luther once lived here; but Christ came and Luther moved out to make room for Him. Now, I no longer live; but Christ liveth in me.'" And Luther was but echoing the feelings of multitudes.

Jesus came to give a new glow to life. The early Christians were easily distinguished from the non-Christians of their day by their shining faces. Especially was that seen when loved ones were snatched from their midst, or when they calmly faced death at the hands of their persecutors. But the distinguishing glow came because He had taken possession of their hearts. It is well for us to consider what takes place when Jesus is earnestly accepted.

In the first place, a life of constant, uninterrupted fellowship begins with Him. This is the secret of victorious living. He said life was following Him. This was the invitation He issued throughout His ministry when He called men unto a new life. He made clear that following Him was not a hobby. It was not something to be done when there was nothing else to do, or when in their exhaustion they turned to Him

LIFE BEGINS WITH JESUS

for a few moments of relaxation. That was not constant, uninterrupted fellowship. Following Him is a challenging adventure. It is not only a full time job, but it must continue in every experience and every avenue of endeavor. Neither is it tame, unexciting business. It should produce a way of life that is both startling and daring. "God calls," exclaimed George Hodges. "It is better to obey blunderingly than not to obey at all!" "Yes," we reply, "we know and we have blundered." But that shouldn't cause us to hesitate. We can be sure that He, who was surrounded by impulsive, faltering disciples, understands and gives us full credit for our desires as well as our service.

Every so often the world is startled, not only by the message, but also the daring of some flaming messenger of God. Every reformer has produced that effect upon his age. They have not been understood or accepted any more than was the One they proclaimed. This was so common in the early days of Christianity that every Christian was considered a disturber.

The disciples soon caught this spirit and it made them realize the significance of their ministry. When He first called them He said, "Follow me and I will make you fishers of men." That required a greater skill and daring than braving the dangers of a temperamental sea to cast their nets for fish. Yet these startling words gripped them and they responded, not to the easy but the hard. "Ye are the light of the world," He reminded them. That was startling indeed. These common, ordinary, everyday men, suddenly rose from obscurity to become the light of the world. "Ye are the salt of the earth," He continued, and they who knew the value of salt and what it meant to their day, were not slow to understand what was expected of them. "Ye shall be witnesses unto me," He said later. Startling, because they became aware their greatest work was to begin the moment He ascended unto His Father. But notice that in all this they were not to work alone. "Lo, I am with you alway." Theirs was to be a life of constant, uninterrupted fellowship with Him.

Even though the Master is with us in all our varied experiences much is required on our part. Following Him is strenuous travel and life's burdens do not make it easier. It means perseverance. There are many places we would desire to stop. How nice if someone would step in and share the load that is ours. Or like Peter on the Mount of Transfiguration, we, too, will come to a desired haven, and be tempted to say, "Master it is good for us to be here."

Joanne has been staying on the mainland this winter with her little two and a half year old cousin, Linda Lee. Linda often experiences difficulty drinking water, due to a slight impatience on her part to get at the rest of the food. This is usually attended by considerable coughing. On one occasion, when I visited them, we went to a drug store for ice cream. A large glass of water was brought each, and neither considered they had received their money's worth until the glass as well as the dish was emptied. In her haste, Linda Lee began to cough and sputter as usual. But after each experience, when she regained control of her voice, her little face beamed and she would shout, "It must'a had a

LIFE BEGINS WITH JESUS

bone in it!" A feeling akin to this often comes with following Jesus. We soon realize it has "a bone in it," and it is not the easy, comfortable thing we imagined, but we must go on. We are following Him and His path always leads where problems, difficulties and obstacles are most pronounced. The enticing mountain top is meant only to provide strength for the harrowing events that follow. To persevere requires more than defensive maneuvers. A defensive mood is not only easier for the enemy to destroy, but it usually indicates a back solidly against the wall, waging a last stand fight. Jesus took the initiative and His commands were always a challenge to advance. It was the offensive He stressed and that is the prelude to victory.

In the second place, the abundant life begins with Jesus. It is a moving picture the Gospels give of His life. Although He was never flustered or unduly hurried, He is always hastening to help people. Still-life had little place in His ministry, and the end of all this was to bestow a more abundant life. And why not? He knew the high value God placed upon every child of His, even the most unworthy. That is the reason Jesus stressed the need of forgiveness. "Sin destroys," He kept repeating, "but I am come to seek and to save and only through salvation can the abundant life be secured."

The Apostle Paul realized how precious we are in the sight of God. We are His special treasure, He suggests. Then God is wealthy because of us! And we have gone through life thinking that we were just another insignificant person like millions more who

LIFE BEGINS WITH JESUS

dot the earth. We still sing hymns that speak of us as worms. Worms? "How ridiculous!" exclaims the Psalmist, "why, we are a little lower than the angels." And John says, "Now are we the sons of God." Yes, we are His special treasure; the most valuable possession He has. No wonder He sent Jesus to redeem us! Can we continue on our way as broken, beaten individuals, considering ourselves as unimportant? God is more careful with His treasure than we are with ours, and the richer we make Him by the beauty of our lives, the greater becomes the treasure we cannot lose. Heaven is a richer place this moment because of us, and the treasures we have deposited with Him, making it that, will be ours through eternity. That is what Jesus had in mind when He said, "Lay up for yourselves treasures in heaven, where neither moth nor rust doth corrupt and where thieves do not break through nor steal; for where your treasure is, there will your heart be also." That is the abundant life.

The abundant life is the tonic we need for lowered spiritual vitality. When faith grows dim, when hope wanes and we begin to sag, there is something wrong. In such a world as this, with war in our front yard, we need all the spiritual strength available. Jesus has every vital vitamin necessary, and they are as potent this moment as in the day He first revealed an inexhaustible supply. If we begin to wilt and doubt their value for this crisis, let us look back to the day when they were first tried. If they were sufficient for the hectic, cruel, trying years following Pentecost, we have no reason to question their potency for this hour. Increased resist-

LIFE BEGINS WITH JESUS

ance is our need and that gives us power to meet and conquer life. And Christ leads the way. He conquered and that which empowered Him He offers us.

These claims that leap from the pages of the New Testament, telling of changed lives and seemingly miraculous power, are not extravagant. They are the result of abundant living. Whoever receives life from Jesus cannot rest until He brings the Life Giver to others. We are judged by our effectiveness and measured by that to which we are alive. Unless we are aware of the needs of others and deeply concerned for their welfare we cannot expect the same results that attended the ministry of the Apostles. The closer we draw to the Master, the nearer we come to our fellowmen. It is in Him we see what God wants us to be and what He wants us to do in the building of His kingdom.

Our life and ministry are also judged on the basis of what we make alive. We cannot read the life of Jesus without becoming aware that He is either teaching, healing, seeking the lost or visiting some place of mourning, and the purpose was to give life.

In the third place, a life of unshaken faith begins with Jesus. That was the faith He had in God. All the childlike characteristics He insisted His followers must have if they are to enter Heaven are to be found in Him. It was a deep, beautiful, unbroken faith He possessed, childlike in its simplicity, and so natural and compelling that when He finished talking about God, eyes unconsciously turned upward expecting to see Him.

War is not poetry, yet great poems have been born

LIFE BEGINS WITH JESUS

amidst its sordid surroundings. One has already come from the present conflict and, in the exhibit of "Poems of Faith and Freedom," recently opened in the Library of Congress in Washington, was awarded a place with Rupert Brooke's "The Soldier" and John McCrae's "In Flanders Field," which are masterpieces of the last war. Archibald MacLeish and Joseph Auslander, noted poets and Library of Congress officials, selected it for this honor. The poem is entitled "High Flight" and was written by John Gillespie Magee, Jr., a nineteen year old Pilot Officer who was killed in action December 11, 1941, while serving with the R.C.A.F in England.

John, the son of a former missionary in China, was born in Shanghai. His education was received at Rugby, in England, and Avon Old Farms School in Connecticut. While at the latter institution, and still in his early teens, he published a volume of poems. It was with amazement that I read the little volume, for it seemed impossible that a boy so young could possess such unusual insight and ability.

Instead of going to Yale, as he had planned, he enlisted in the Canadian Air Force. While in training he wrote to a friend, "I have found my place in the sun! I am finding that flying has really been in my blood all the time and I didn't know it   I am rather afraid that I shall emerge from this war as a hopeless illiterate, but it seems so unimportant now   we have each a definite urge to leave our impress on the firmament, if only as a black smudge while spinning to earth for the last time."

The poem was started at an altitude of thirty thou-

LIFE BEGINS WITH JESUS

sand feet on September 3, 1941, and finished shortly after he grounded his plane, and is as follows:

Oh! I have slipped the surly bonds of earth
    And danced the skies on laughter-silvered wings;
Sunward I've climbed, and joined the tumbling mirth
    Of sun-split clouds — and done a hundred things
You have not dreamed of — wheeled and soared and swung
    High in the sunlit silence. Hov'ring there,
I've chased the shouting wind along, and flung
    My eager craft through footless halls of air.

Up, up the long, delirious, burning blue
    I've topped the wind-swept heights with easy grace
Where never lark, or even eagle flew —
And, while with silent lifting mind I've trod
    The high untrespassed sanctity of space,
Put out my hand and touched the face of God.

The faith Jesus possessed was such that He could continually put out His hand and touch the face of God, and it is that faith we need in these trying, uncertain hours. It begins with Him and cannot be experienced apart from the same constant, intimate, uninterrupted fellowship He shared with the Father.

Jesus also had faith in His own power. On one occasion He said, "And I, if I be lifted up from the earth, will draw all men unto me." He was sure of that, so sure that Calvary did not impress Him as a dread, painful experience looming in a darkened future, but as an opportunity. He who was so concerned with the souls of men was not dismayed at the prospect of a cross. His amazing faith would not permit that. The hatred of the world and the unscrupulous conniving of its leaders only increased His desire to continue the

LIFE BEGINS WITH JESUS

work God depended upon Him to complete. The grim-looking future with its long hours of agony and abuse was a challenge; an opportunity to prove His faith was not in vain.

And what faith He has in us! The people of His day marveled and so do we. When He said to the sinful, "Arise, go in peace, and sin no more," He had faith that they would do it. We never find Him snooping around a day or two later to determine how they were living. When He walked from their presence He didn't so much as look back. He had faith in them, even the worst. Neither do we discover Him questioning the value of what He had done or was about to do. It was His unquenchable faith in man that caused Him to accept cheerfully and without quibbling every sacrifice necessary for their salvation. His disciples were a sorry looking lot in the eyes of His critics, but Jesus merely said, "Follow me," and He had faith that they would. And when He finally turned His face toward Jerusalem, He was confident they would follow Him even there. That is the faith He still has in humanity. He never relinquished the trust He had in the best or the unfailing belief that salvation could come to the worst.

In the fourth place, a life of satisfying assurance begins with Jesus. When the clouds begin to gather suggesting impending disaster, we desire above all else someone upon whom we can lean. We can face life as courageously as man has ever faced it, however bleak or discouraging, if we have assurance that strength will be provided. That which prostrates us is the result of

LIFE BEGINS WITH JESUS

meeting it unprepared and attempting to brave it alone. Gray, despondent, lonely days are exceedingly burdensome,

And yet these days of dreariness are sent us from above;
They do not come in anger, but in faithfulness and love;
They come to teach us lessons which bright ones could not yield,
And to leave us blest and thankful when their purpose is revealed.

Whenever victory seems impossible in our life it is time to try Jesus; to trust His word; to have the same faith in Him He has in us. It is then we find not only strength to overcome, but the assurance that that which we feared most has added much to our life. It requires little faith to face the future when we see clearly, but when our vision is blurred or the future takes on alarming shadows it necessitates both courage and faith to move steadily forward. Then it is that Christ assures us we are not alone, and that makes for life. He will sustain us in our hour of need and support us when we stumble.

Years ago an English artist painted a picture called, "The Comforter." It portrays a scene known so well by those who have helplessly watched the passing of a loved one. A young man is seen sitting beside a bed, agony stamped upon his drawn face, looking intently for the last time upon his dying wife. But he is not alone. Seated by his side, though unseen, is another Figure dressed in white. The pierced hands of the silent Presence reach out and hold those of the young man. It is the Comforter, the Lord of Life, fulfilling

LIFE BEGINS WITH JESUS

His promise, "I will not leave you comfortless, I will come to you." Yes, we know and understand, we who have felt His presence when that experience came to us. We were not alone, then, either. Holding our hands in His, reassuring and sustaining us, was the Christ who never leaves nor forsakes His own.

Finally, Eternal Life begins with Jesus. He did more than draw back the curtain and by way of word pictures reveal what was beyond. That would have been sufficient, but it was only the first step in the great unveiling. By way of the resurrection He demonstrated what He said to be true. And perhaps words were not enough; they would not have satisfied. The despair of His own disciples following the crucifixion illustrates how quickly words are forgotten. And we can understand. What tragedy can equal that which comes when a loved one is suddenly snatched from our midst? Especially when youth is still in bloom and strength has seemingly returned. This was the experience of the disciples. They had lived with Jesus, walked with Him, and worked with Him. The most elaborate plans were drawn for the redemption of the race. Then, when He seemed the strongest and His future brightest, Calvary intervened. That moment, in spite of His teachings, they found it impossible to banish from their weary minds the thought that He had gone; that they had lost Him. But with the dawn of the resurrection all this was changed. It was then they remembered His words. Death had not separated them but brought Him nearer. And so it is with our loved ones. "I thank Thee, O Father," prayed George Matheson, "that

LIFE BEGINS WITH JESUS

there is a voice within me which contradicts the silence of death." And our own who have been called aside are not lost, but only a few steps ahead waiting for us to catch up. In the meantime their silent ministry continues. Every obstruction life raised, narrowing the service love urged them to perform, has been removed. It was expedient for them also to go away, that they might draw nearer and complete what upon earth was impossible. The following poem, "Heaven," was written by me some time ago:

> Earth with its beauty may ever attract us;
> Earth with its sorrows give birth to despair;
> Yet we will learn how unchanging is Heaven,
> When we shall claim our inheritance there:
> Living consistently,
> Free from all care.
>
> Sweet our reception by earth, yet far sweeter
> Will be our welcome on that Golden Shore;
> City of promise, where loved ones await us
> As we debark when life's journey is o'er:
> Living triumphantly,
> Peace evermore.
>
> Drear is earth's valley and dark is its shadow,
> Unlike the Land that destroyeth all fears;
> City of comfort, where death never enters,
> Sorrow is barred, and where falleth no tears:
> Living constructively,
> Down through the years.
>
> Hail to that City our Father prepareth,
> Dear to our soul though concealed from our sight;
> City of refuge, our home through the ages,
> Dwelling with Jesus who giveth it light:
> Living eternally,
> Knowing no night.

This is the life that begins with Jesus.

WHAT WE NEED MOST

"Take my yoke upon you for my yoke is easy, and my burden is light." — MATTHEW 11:29-30

WHAT A MAN! The more we study His words the less we wonder why the people who first heard them listened in amazement. "Turn the other cheek Go an extra mile   Enter in at the straight gate. Deny thyself   Sell what thou hast and give to the poor   Take up the cross and follow me." Even today men listen and then make every conceivable attempt to evade His requirements. The text of our sermon appears to be a staggering claim. If we were weary, ready to fall under our burden, and the friend from whom we sought advice said, "Why man, what you need is a yoke," what would we say?

When these words were spoken, Jesus was addressing a group of men and women who were discouraged, disheartened and bewildered. The little world that was once so bright for some had suddenly become darkened. Ominous shadows were settling upon others. They wanted to see the sunshine again, regain the peace and contentment they had lost, and above all find some avenue of escape. Yet to them Jesus said, "Life for you begins with a yoke." That in itself was amazing, but was only half the picture. The other half rested in Jesus. It was the hour of disappointment and discouragement for Him. The enthusiasm of many would-be followers had begun to wane. He was facing bitter opposition from those in power. Although His name had been carried into every section touched by His ministry, unkind, biting, slanderous words had likewise traveled the same area. Yet in the face of this, He said, "My yoke is easy; my burden is light."

No matter how we view these words one thing is certain, yokes are inevitable. We cannot escape them. Even the weary multitude must have realized that. They knew, too, that Jesus was not offering any yoke, for they understood Him to the extent that He would not call them from one hard to bear to another that would be harder. Neither would He add to their overloaded lives. They knew, because it was "My yoke" He offered; not another oppressive burden suddenly and unexpectedly clamped upon them by the world. Amazing, of course, yet not so startling in the light of His life and ministry. There was a difference and that difference was in the person issuing the invitation.

Life is impossible apart from yokes. God knew that long before we did, therefore He made us yoke bearers. Our ability to "snap out of it" after life has slipped upon us a yoke is not accidental. We were created for that purpose. Defeats, failures, misunderstanding, abuse, trouble, all are burdens that we feel, yet we get over them. We do not succumb. "The tests of life," says Maltbie D. Babcock, "are to make, not break us." And they will make us if we allow them that opportunity. Even the ordinary duties place heavy loads upon us. To follow a mother for one day is to gain a new insight into her responsibilities, yet mothers survive and keep cheerful. The road of fatherhood is not one that leads by still waters. Earning a living is not a trivial matter. The pressure of business,

WHAT WE NEED MOST

financial worries, and the thought of safeguarding the family is a tremendous strain. Yet fathers continue to labor and find a joy in doing just that. God never intended life to be easy and for that reason made us to stand almost superhuman pressure.

While on his sick bed Martin Luther said, "These pains and troubles here are like the type the printers set; as they look now, we have to read them backwards, and they seem to have no sense or meaning in them; but up yonder, when the Lord God prints us off in the life to come, we shall find they make brave reading." And brave reading they will make, these lives of ours, dashed upon the jagged rocks of tragedy one day, courageously rising, prepared to face whatever else might come the next. We might go limping, bleeding, staggering half dazedly through the weeks that follow, but we do not stop.

Is not that the reason we become restless when the yoke is removed? Have you watched a man the first weeks after he has retired from business? He has looked forward to that day for years, now it has come, and he is the most restless person on his street. He doesn't know what to do with his time. His extreme restlessness becomes a burden to those who love him most.

We are wrong when we speak of the relief that comes when a bedridden loved one has suddenly been called to a new home. The yoke of patient ministry that has been gladly borne through the months, even years, of illness is not easily forgotten when removed. Love that gives grows stronger with the days, and when we are relieved of that responsibility we become crushed and our hearts broken.

Although we are made to bear yokes it was not intended that we should bear them alone. There are times when the responsibility of a mother would be impossible were it not for the comfort and help of the one sharing life with her. And the sympathy, understanding, and encouragement of the wife keeps the father at his task. Our hearts always ache for the wife or husband who is forced to bear their burdens alone. I remember reading a letter some time ago from a young mother who had just given birth to a baby. In the letter she made one reference to her husband in these words, "He is out somewhere tonight and only God knows what woman he is with." How deeply we feel the pain suffered by that poor soul forced as she was to bear life's heaviest burdens alone.

In life's varied experiences God intended that we should have yoke-fellows, but He didn't stop there. He meant us to be yoke-fellows with a life higher than our own—with Him, and with His Son. That is what Jesus meant when He said, "Take my yoke upon you." He was not adding another burden but was seeking to relieve us by offering to share what we could not carry alone.

When we consider this invitation we make amazing discoveries. In the first place, being a yoke-fellow with Him is a necessity. It is a necessity from our point of view as well as His. Who hasn't felt the yoke of pain, especially if that pain indicates trouble ahead? If we face the possibility of extended suffering, we need

WHAT WE NEED MOST

a companion stronger than the human. The Apostles conquered in the midst of relentless persecution because they were yoked with Jesus.

What shall we say for the yoke of blasted hopes? Every life can write its own volume on this subject. The tragedy is that many of our hopes are blasted at the time we thought they would be fulfilled. Hopes that have centered around a happy home have suddenly ended. Our hopes center in so many things, and when they are destroyed we ask what is left. More than we are aware of at this moment, if Christ is our yoke-fellow.

> "The cross is too great!" I cried —
> "More than the back can bear;
> So rough and heavy and wide,
> And nobody by to care!"
> And One stooped softly and touched my hand:
> "I know. I care. And I understand."

No one escapes the yoke of sorrow. Only recently there appeared a news item following the funeral of a woman in England. It said that the blinds of her house were raised for the first time in twenty-five years. Some of the older people knew the reason, but the younger generation only wondered. Her passing recalled what had long been kept secret. Twenty-five years before, her daughter died. She pulled down the curtains at that time and had lived in darkness ever since. Poor, misguided soul! She evidently had never become a yoke-fellow with Jesus. For twenty-five years she bore her sorrow alone. If there is ever a time we need to take the yoke of Christ, it is then. That is the only

LIFE BEGINS WITH JESUS

thing that will raise the blinds that have suddenly descended upon our lives. A yoke is necessary if we expect to meet the challenge of life.

In the second place, His yoke is not of one design. Designs and patterns go out of style with the years. Styles change with amazing rapidity, yet the yoke of Christ is never out of date. It fits today as perfectly as it did the day He ministered. That will be the story two thousand years hence, because His yoke fits every need, and human needs never change. People laughed and rejoiced in His day. Tears revealed every heartbreaking experience felt today. Poverty caused the same distress, sickness the same pain, sin the same destruction, and life its endless problems. The yoke of the Master was designed for these needs, and is adjusted to each individual life. We classify people as Christians or non-Christians, citizens or aliens, learned or unlearned, rich or poor, righteous or unrighteous. This is a broad classification, and the difference within each group is as pronounced as darkness and light. Jesus dealt in terms of one, and that is always the secret of perfect fit.

In the third place, the yoke of the Master was padded. How our hearts leap at that! It was not meant to chafe. Chafing comes with a poor fit and attempting to pull alone. This only adds to our misery. Let us not forget that the padding is meant for a purpose.

His yoke is padded with love. Are not our burdens easier to bear when love is present? That is what Christ offers with His yoke. If human love doesn't count the cost, we can be sure His does. Human love

WHAT WE NEED MOST

might fail even in the dreary hours of life, but His is undying.

His yoke is padded with understanding. He knows our needs and is ever aware of our problems. He understands us and understanding and love are bosom companions. We look with distrust and envy upon our fellowmen because we do not know them. We do not view our loved ones in the same light for we have seen in them what no one else has. While others might like them, we love them, all because we so thoroughly understand them.

His yoke is padded with patience. How impatient we sometimes become! Our impatience often centers around those who are pulling a tremendous load. We are not always Christ-like in this respect. Who could have been as patient with the impulsive Peter as Jesus, yet how great the reward! How patient He was with those who didn't understand! When the disciples grew impatient with the multitude and wanted to send them away, He fed them. When many who had walked with Him suddenly left, Jesus merely said to His disciples, "Will ye also go away?" What hope there is in Christ! Though we fret under our yoke, He never lacks patience with us. He still stands ready to share the heaviest load life lays upon us.

His yoke is also padded with gentleness. It is a kindly yoke. He who was was so kind and gentle with little children, the sinful, those diseased in mind and body, is still the same in His dealings with us. Christ has not changed. His yoke is not a weight. It is not an instrument of punishment. It is padded with gentleness for our comfort.

Again, His yoke sustains us. Strange, isn't it, that a yoke should be the means of our salvation! Yet, this is what it is. It is like a hand extended to lift us up. We cannot succumb when we are yoked with Him. His yoke sustains because it keeps us in step with Him. When oxen are yoked together they walk together. One is not limping alone down the road. They remain side by side as long as the yoke is intact. When we are yoked with Jesus our limping days are over. That is a great blessing in a day when so much of the world is out of step. It is a tragedy when a Christian is out of harmony with Christ. We have witnessed that in the realm of religion. Many sincere but misguided souls who feel they have the only truth are often so out of step with the Christ of the Gospels that their hot, flustered, frenzied attempt to convince, and their violent denunciations of those unmoved by their expositions, are pathetic. They march by only one tune, yet the Saviour was a master of melodies.

His yoke sustains us because it gives direction to life. We can be in step with someone yet go in the wrong direction. Life is full of highways. This is the reason so many of us become confused and lose our way. But the Master knows where He is going, and also the direction we should take. There are no questions when we are yoked with Him because we go with Him. As I was seated near the Deaconess Hospital in Boston last summer, a lad approached, tears in his eyes, sobbing aloud. I said, "What's wrong, sonny?" The

WHAT WE NEED MOST

reply was, "I'm lost." He eagerly drew close to me. It's a terrible feeling to be lost. I had the same feeling in my heart, for I knew what would soon happen in that hospital. I asked him what street he wanted and then pointed out the direction, but he turned a sad face to me and said, "Mister, maybe I won't find it. Won't you walk there with me?" Isn't that the feeling we all have? It is not enough for someone to point out the direction. We want one who will go with us. That is what Jesus does. For when we are yoked with Him He does more than point. We walk that road together. "With a loved presence by my side the long way is made short, the muddy way is made clean," said George Matheson. And so it is. We who have walked by the side of a loved one never noticed the distance or became conscious of the dirt. It is when they leave us, and we walk without them, that the road seems long and steep. It is then Jesus whispers, "Take my yoke upon you. We will walk it out together." Ethel Maude Colson has presented the difference separation makes in the following poem:

Since she went — home —
    The saddened world has never seemed so bright;
    There is less splendor in the morning's light
        And duller now the radiant moonbeams shine.
    All nature's joys come now to slower birth,
    And thou hast lost, O tender morning earth,
        The glory that was thine!

Since she went — home —
    The dragging days seem now so drear and long;
    A hint of sadness chills the gayest song,
        A plaintive tone in every sound I hear,

LIFE BEGINS WITH JESUS

> Even the sunlight's rays of purest gold,
> Like all the world, seem something dull and cold,
>   Missing her presence dear
> Since she went — home —
>   So large a world to lose so very much,
>   In one small woman's face and voice and touch,
>   The simple magic of her tender smile!
>   So full a world to have so empty grown
>   For one small woman's quiet soul and tone,
>   And yet—'twill empty be for such a while
>   Since she went — home!

He sustains by steadying us. How we need this in our day! We become unnerved and unsteady by the slaughter that consumes so much of the world, turning fearful faces towards the sky, not knowing when we will be next. We become faint, ready to fall, when many of the tragic experiences already alluded to in this sermon come our way. Life is crowded with hours that call for a stronger hand to hold and guide us.

> I have been through the valley of weeping,
>   The valley of sorrow and pain;
> But the "God of all comfort" was with me,
>   At hand to uphold and sustain.

That hand reaches out for ours, even in the dark. When an ox becomes weary, does not the yoke that likewise is upon his yoke-fellow steady him? To even a greater extent is that true of our Divine Partner, who keeps us from falling, and helps us over the rough, dangerous ground.

Who are the happiest people? The world would reply, "The care free, the reckless, the wealthy, the pleasure devotees." But are they? Have you read the

WHAT WE NEED MOST

letters of Paul recently? If so, you will find the answer. Paul had none of the world's ease after he gave himself to Christ. Bruised, beaten, stoned, persecuted, imprisoned, yet one of the happiest men who ever lived. And the secret? He was a yoke-fellow with Christ.

Everything said of Paul is true of the great Christians of all ages. Their happiness did not come from the world with its broad avenues of death and distruction. They repudiated all that and suffered as a result. The hour that called for a song from the lips of the Master came when He left behind the seclusion of the upper room for a cross. And the happy people you know? Are they not those who are yoke-fellows with Him?

May we end our search for peace and contentment in the areas of life in which they cannot be found. The answer is in our text, "Take my yoke upon you." That is the secret of happiness. That is the only means whereby the city of God can be reached.

CONQUERORS, PLUS

"In all these things we are more than conquerors, through him that loved us." — ROMANS 8:37

THE ABOVE text sounds like the words of a professional boaster. One a little better and a little more experienced than the rest. Yet think of the little half-blind man who uttered them! Compare him to the ruthless warriors of his day. Would he be looked upon as a conqueror? Beaten, stoned, left for dead, persecuted unmercifully, nevertheless daring to cry aloud, "We are more than conquerors." How foolish his words must have sounded, especially to those to whom they were addressed. Yet he was right. This was not an idle boast. He was giving expression to that which he had experienced. He knew that final victory was impossible to those who made no strategic plans for inward conquest.

There are three ways in which we can face life with all its varied and trying experiences. The first is to meekly accept defeat, to succumb, to allow the experiences of life to overwhelm us. It is possible for defeat to come from many unexpected directions.

To be defeated could mean remaining indifferent. The two who made no attempt to aid the poor wounded man lying by the roadside in the parable of the Good Samaritan have been unrelentlessly condemned. Yet they did nothing to injure him further. They merely passed by on the other side, but that was injury enough. It reveals their callousness and indifference to another's suffering. Whenever we become indifferent to that which will help our fellowmen or relieve their suffering, we are less than conquerors. Whenever we refuse to help kingdom causes or back the onward progress of Christ, we indicate our willingness to accept defeat. Victory is impossible to one indifferent to anything advocated by the Master.

We are defeated when we attempt to flee from life. To live victoriously is not always easy. Life's experiences are often bitter, but running away is not the remedy. God once called a man to minister in a hard field. After hasty consideration of the command he decided not to obey. He didn't like this city. He cared less for the people. He was unwilling to face the hard problems that were before him, so he became a fugitive. In so doing he considered himself smart, but Jonah soon learned that running away from a bad experience was impossible. Impossible, because he couldn't run away from his conscience or the Eternal. As the man who seeks to run away from life by way of narcotics and drink, he realizes upon coming to himself that he is back where he was, plus a headache and a habit almost impossible to break. Turlough O'Corolan, Irish poet and musician of the eighteenth century, pressed a bowl of wine to his dying lips, saying, "It would be hard indeed if we two friends should part after so many years without one sweet kiss." A man is known by his habits and desires as well as by his friends. This is the expression of one whose habits, desires, and friends were the result of continued fleeing from life's unwelcome experiences. An endeavor to flee indicates defeat.

We are already defeated whenever we express a willingness to turn ourselves over to the enemy. In so doing we have made an unconditional surrender. What

CONQUERORS, PLUS

is the use of fighting any longer? Why be good? Why be faithful? It isn't worth it, we argue, so we hoist the white flag. This is the way Judas reasoned. Why continue to follow one who refused to be made king and set up a kingdom of plenty? He had served Jesus long enough, and yet what was he to receive? Some vague kingdom of the future! That wasn't what he wanted. He desired a kingdom now, and it was becoming increasingly evident that this was not the Master's plan, so he turned everything, including Christ and himself, over to the forces of unrighteousness.

Men still reason as Judas did. To what advantage is happiness that looms in the future? They demand happiness now, and that God seems to deny. Therefore, why follow Him? Why not forsake Him and turn to the world? they conclude. Live today, never mind tomorrow! "There is nothing that a man can less afford to leave at home," warned Richardson Packe, "than his conscience or his good habits." And bitter, painful experiences have taught us the truth of this statement. Whenever we become submissive to the forces arrayed against Christ, regardless of the reason, we have met defeat.

The fourth way to meet defeat is to be conquered. Whether we turn to the enemy, or allow him to rush in and capture us, the result is the same. We are defeated and as such can momentarily become slaves. Yet more credit is to be bestowed upon the person who makes an attempt to stand, however feeble his fighting qualities are. The moment we lose faith in God, defeat seems imminent. Whenever we allow sin to assume

LIFE BEGINS WITH JESUS

mastery of our lives, slavery begins. Demas was an impressive young leader of the early church. But he allowed his faith to wane, looked longingly in the direction of the world, was fascinated by the outward show of the forces long considered as the enemy, and he ceased fighting. We are less than a conqueror when we permit any force foreign to God or Christianity to conquer us. "The violence done us by others," said La Rochefoucauld, "is often less painful than that which we do to ourselves." If the volume of our life as God reads it could be opened to public view, our fellowmen would be amazed to read how personal and intimate our "enemy" actually was. And that which is true of us can with equal certainty be said of them.

The second way to face life is to be a conqueror and nothing more. Dictators have been conquerors for awhile, due to their unscrupulous methods, falsehoods, fiendish cruelty, regimentation, and treacherous assaults. But it is impossible for them to be more than that because their underlying principles are all wrong. They conquer at the price of their own soul.

Life is full of individuals who can never rise above the level of mere conquest. Some have advanced to unprecedented heights in the material realm and have reaped a financial harvest. Others have rocketed in various fields of endeavor and have achieved fame. Yet the tragedy is that a great proportion are conquerors only because they have gained no victories in the realm of the spirit. The names of many who could be great will never be known, even though they have done some brave living and attained a fair amount of success, be-

CONQUERORS, PLUS

cause, unfortunately, they did not continue their advance. Sometime ago I talked with a man who said he lived a good life because it paid. He was not religious and cared little for the church, yet it paid him dividends to be good. Even though such a life might appeal, he could never rise above the average for his motives were selfish. His good life was lived because success and profits depended upon it.

To be a conqueror is better than to fall short, but is not enough. Many can live through a horrible experience, yet not be made any bigger or better because of it. Others can overcome the fears that visit every life, but succumb to the lusts of the flesh. History records not only the great, but the tyrants who could not die happy unless inflicting torture on others. "My philosophy is worn out by suffering," confessed Frederick the Great. "I am no saint, like those of whom we read in the legends; and I will own that I should die content if only I could first inflict a portion of the misery which I endure." We would not expect anything else from a life whose ambition it was to enslave nations and inflict torture upon the helpless multitudes. No one can become more than a conqueror who has not made an attempt to be as successful spiritually as he has physically and materially.

The third way to face life is to be a conqueror, plus. That is what the Apostle Paul is saying in our text. A victory is not enough. We must do something with it after it is won.

First, we are more than conquerors when we refuse to lower our ideals in the face of opposition. The ideals

LIFE BEGINS WITH JESUS

of Jesus have never been surpassed. They never will, yet He was terribly criticized. Every time He emphasized a truth, opposition mounted. The teachings we admire most made Him hated by the multitudes who listened as He first gave them expression. Yet in the face of this rising opposition Jesus remained steadfast. His ideals grew; they did not diminish. Every step nearer the cross caused Him to loom bigger upon the horizon of His day. And we are more than conquerors when we assume ideals worthy of a Christian and maintain them at all costs.

We are more than conquerors when we deny self in the midst of selfishness. The fact that Jesus insisted upon this doesn't make it easy. Nothing is easy that calls for stern denial. Especially is this true here, for we have a tendency to pamper ourselves. Yet Jesus insisted we must say "No" to self before we were prepared to take the cross and follow Him. To do that would make us conquerors, plus. Jesus faced the prevailing selfishness of His day. Every age has faced it, and we do today. In such surroundings the person who denies self seems out of place, appears to be so old-fashioned. It is for this reason the "plus" is exceedingly hard to attach. When we learn to say "No" to our worldly ambitions, the desires of the flesh, the shady, twisting road to material gain—to anything not in harmony with Christ—then we become more than conquerors.

We are more than conquerors when we achieve victory in the presence of apparent defeat. Whatever else is lost, we must courageously hold everything vir-

CONQUERORS, PLUS

tuous. We have already considered directions leading to defeat. Each of the roads suggested have been traveled when victory could have easily been attained. The thought now is different. It is adding the "plus" to life when the "minus" sign is greatly enlarged and heavily underlined. Life bombards us incessantly with forces that would subdue and defeat us. Their appeal is to every area of our life. The struggle is often intense, but as Christians we are pledged to victory, not defeat. Like the Apostles we must go forward. That makes us more than conquerors.

We are more than conquerors when we go the extra mile. The first mile makes us conquerors; the second adds the "plus." This is hard. When our brother has offended us, how easy it is to leave him! When we have done our duty, how difficult to continue knowing that others are neglecting theirs! The extra mile is harder to travel than the many that precede. Jesus recognized this when He preached it. Yet it is a divine requirement and the Christian life is judged on the basis of the second mile, not the first. "It is the extra mile that makes the Christian; the measured mile makes the Pharisee," so said Samuel Chadwick. And Jesus condemned the Pharisaic attitude saying, "Except your righteousness shall exceed the righteousness of the scribes and Pharisees, ye shall in no case enter into the kingdom of heaven." The first is the distance every conqueror goes; the second is the distance traveled by conquerors, plus.

To love and forgive when hated and wronged makes us more than conquerors. This is exceedingly difficult. Can we extend the hand of forgiveness when wronged, or return love after being the recipients of hate? This question is not easy, yet in view of the Master's teaching on the subject some satisfactory answer must be made. He not only loved His enemies and taught His disciples to do the same, but He never held grievances, and His prayer of forgiveness during the crucifixion was for those who had wronged Him most. This does not mean that they beheld His God-like qualities or appreciated His sacrifice to such an extent that hate ceased and His many prayers for them were answered.

To love and forgive doesn't mean that we should not defend ourselves against charges that are false. Jesus had occasion to, many times, yet He never lost His desire to save the offenders. He did not grow bitter or resort to their tactics. The defense of Himself was always coupled with a warning of inevitable destruction of the wrongdoer unless He repented. To be a conqueror, plus, does not take away any God-given right, but it does remove every desire to be as hateful, mean, and cruel, as those governed by the base ideals of the world.

We are more than conquerors when we dare to place our most treasured possessions in the Master's arms and leave them there. This is extremely hard, but the road to conquest is never easy. We may proceed haltingly and even blunderingly. Perhaps we will stumble to our knees, but that only sends us rushing to the Master, seeking strength and guidance, and entering into a covenant with Him: that no matter how complete or

CONQUERORS, PLUS

devastating our experience, we will not allow it to hold our shoulders to the ground.

The fear of separation, with its seemingly unbearable inward pain and unceasing loneliness, makes it hard, tremendously hard, to leave our own even with Him. We will gladly do anything, we say, to retain them, and we mean it. God intended that we should. We would exchange places with them during their suffering, and now, even now, we would cheerfully do the same. Who hasn't understood and keenly felt the words of David's lamentation over his dead son? "O my son Absalom, my son, my son Absalom! would God I had died for thee, O Absalom, my son, my son!" His sobs break the silence created by the tragedy and his quivering body refuses to be steadied.

But separation is not as complete as we suppose. Our fears are not entirely grounded. "Who shall separate us from the love of Christ?" asks the Apostle Paul only a moment before he penned the words of our text. He then named the common fears of mankind, and shouted exultingly that they were powerless to remove us from His presence. And if they cannot separate us from Him, neither can they from those we love. Not even death, that which we dread the most, he says, can separate us from the love of God in Christ Jesus.

Two weeks ago today I followed my wife from the church in which we were married only ten years ago to the family lot in a near-by quiet, peaceful cemetery. But there is a joy in my heart, and has been for some days, for I know that her final resting place is not where we laid her.

LIFE BEGINS WITH JESUS

> She did not die;
> She was too near an angel.
> One morn near break of day,
> Hand in hand with some unseen evangel,
> She went away.

Yet in spite of this departure I have the firm assurance that she is still with me, carrying on the tender ministry so near to her heart. Of course, she is in the Father's House, but why do we feel that because our loved ones are there, it is impossible for them to be with us? That is not the conception we have of Jesus, yet is He not in the Father's House? We feel His presence, we know He sees, understands, and ministers to us continually. Would our own, who are as interested in our welfare as the Master Himself, be deprived of that privilege? Remember, that desire was given them by God, and is so strong, that they hold to it tenaciously despite the efforts of the world to wrest it from them. How unreasonable to think that the One who gave it would remove it at the hour when our broken hearts yearn for it most!

The hand that steadies and comforts us, that seems to possess a power all its own in relieving pain, is never needed as much as now. It was a blessing during the past years. It is a necessity when the lights are dimmed in our home and the fever that burns within continues unchecked. I believe God has an answer for that. Not only does He feel our pain and minister to us through His Son, but He sends the same hands to serve, and the same understanding, sympathetic, beautiful life to bestow upon us her love. As someone has written:

CONQUERORS, PLUS

And still her silent ministry
    Within my heart hath place,
As when on earth she walked with me,
    And met me face to face.
Her life is still forever mine:
    What she to me has been
Hath left henceforth its seal and sign
    Engraven deep within.

Dr. J. D. Jones writes that in *The Life of Alfred Lyttelton* is recorded a tragic experience that came to him as a young man. His beautiful wife, after approximately a year of married life, passed away, leaving him bewildered and crushed. However, she left a will, and in it this touching paragraph concerning her husband: "The sadness of death and parting is greatly lessened to me by the fact of my consciousness of the eternal, indivisable oneness of Alfred and me. I feel as long as he is down here, I must be here, silently, secretly sitting beside him, as I do every evening now, however much my soul is on the other side." That is the desire, the intense yearning of our loved ones, and the God who gave it never intended it to be destroyed. Instead, His plans call for continued development. On the other side, where all of life is enlarged and every worthy ambition increased in effectiveness, the longing of our own to be in our midst where they can guide, protect, minister, advise and unceasingly love, will expand to hitherto undreamed of proportions.

A few verses from a much longer poem entitled, "He and She," by Sir Edwin Arnold, reveals the love — yes, the increased love — that prevails on both sides when this experience comes to a home.

LIFE BEGINS WITH JESUS

"She is dead," they said to him. "Come away;
Kiss her and leave her — thy love is clay!"

But he, who loved her too well to dread
The sweet, the stately, the beautiful dead,

He lit his lamp and took the key
And turned it — alone again — he and she.

Who will believe that he heard her say,
With the sweet, soft voice, in the dear old way,

"The utmost wonder is this — I hear
And see you, and love you, and kiss you, dear.

"I am your angel, who was your bride
And know that, though dead, I have never died."

Finally, how are we to become more than conquerors? It is one thing to suggest what should be done; it is another to determine how we can do it. Paul gives the answer in our text. "We are more than conquerors through Christ," he says. Conquest is impossible apart from Christ the conqueror. This means that He first must conquer us. We must yield ourselves to Him, and by His strength, not ours, victory is gained. Every Christian can add the "plus," if he so desires, because he is empowered by the One who has power.

When we become more than a conqueror through Christ we gain a Companion in victory. We are not alone. The victorious Christ is with us, surrounding us with His love and becoming more intimate with the days. As Christians we cannot go through the fiery furnace of trial or face the sorrows of life without sensing the nearness of this Companion in victory. "I have kept the faith," shouted Paul and well he could, for he

CONQUERORS, PLUS

knew the Companion who was ever by his side. That faith compelled obedience. "I was not disobedient to the heavenly vision," was more than a truth relating to his conversion. It was a record of his life and ministry. He found that faith sufficient for all of life's experiences. He could not keep that to himself as he looked back over the days of his labor. It must be told. Men were stumbling, groping blindly, seeking a way out of their suffering and sorrow. They needed light, but more than that, poor souls, they needed life. Jesus was the answer, this Companion, without whom no troublesome problem could be satisfactorily solved. He had kept faith with the Master, and he could testify how in a greater degree that Companion had kept faith with him.

I do not know what your burdens of the moment are, but you have them and feel their weight even now. Whatever their nature, is not this the time when our Companion in victory is indispensable? "When my schoolroom is darkened," said C. H. Spurgeon, "I see most." Yes, for it is then our eyesight is sharpened and we see more, far more, then we have dreamed possible. And we realize that now we need more of Christ, not less. I am deeply sorry for those who grow bitter or allow the unexpected, difficult situation to turn them away from their only source of comfort. Neither can I understand how anyone can allow their faith to wane at the point where it can mean the most. Will you not, with me, dedicate yourself anew to this conquering Christ, who makes us more than conquerors in every area of life's experiences?

WHAT CHRIST WOULD DO FOR US

"Come unto me, all ye that labour and are heavy laden, and I will give you rest." — MATTHEW 11:28

JESUS WAS a perfect host. He not only issued invitations to all, but those who accepted left His presence richer and stronger. Yet He demanded much from His guests. In this He differs from the host of the modern day. Whenever an invitation is received we know that all required of us is to enjoy ourselves. To be able to say, "I have had a delightful evening," is to place a wreath of smiles on the face of the one who entertained. It is only proper that we should be both courteous and appreciative, even though conscious we have not grown in spirit. Our lack of growth results from the host doing everything possible to make the evening easy and enjoyable. Games are planned in advance and all we do is enjoy them. Refreshments are ready at the proper time and we simply eat and drink. We do not complain for we desire it that way.

We would like to have life as a host play the same part. Ease, comfort, and luxury are what we desire. Freedom from pain, worry, and sorrow should be guaranteed. How many times have we heard others complain that life has been unkind! When we ask "Why?" we discover that it has demanded from them only what it demands from all. Life is not a perfect host as the world expects it to be. It doesn't consist of playing parlor games and providing tempting refreshments. If it did, the world would be full of weak, flabby bodies and deflated souls. We do not know how greatly we sin against ourselves when we ask that life be only kind and good. God knew, and He made life the host that would shape a world worth creating. We make the same demands upon religion. We do not want a religion that will cost. We expect the church to offer something enticing every time an invitation is given. As in the case of life, we want all the benefits and future security religion can provide at the lowest price.

But returning to Jesus, we discover that as a host, He was without equal. The Gospels record His invitations. All are greatly desired, yet when accepted, certain requirements are demanded before the entertainment is provided and the refreshments served.

If we were asked to give our favorite verse of Scripture many of us would repeat the text of this sermon. Youth might not. They haven't labored long enough or felt the weight of burdens to such an extent that they would appreciate these words. They would prefer a challenge to an invitation. Yet I wonder if there is not a challenge here? Perhaps we have allowed the word "rest" to blind us from seeing anything else. Nevertheless, for the great bulk of humanity this text comes as an oasis in a desert; as a land at peace in the midst of a world at war; as a strong arm to lift us up when we are about to go down.

What makes it so precious? If we gave this invitation would mankind flock to us, assured their load would be lifted and a long dreamed of rest given? Hardly! Its tremendous appeal is due to the fact that it was spoken by One divine.

Yet He who called the weary unto Him was weary Himself. How is it possible, then, we ask, that He could give unto others that which He seemed to have lacked? Was He not in need of the rest He freely offered? We recall His confession of having nowhere to lay His head; that even the wild life had more security and worldly comfort than He. In the fourth chapter of John we behold Him, hot, dusty, and perspiring, sitting upon the well in a Samaritan village. Repeatedly He withdrew from the multitude because of weariness. Yet this wearied Christ continued to invite other wearied people unto Him.

And was He not heavy laden? A casual glance immediately reveals the tremendous burdens constantly placed upon Him. He was burdened with the sins of the world, the sickness, poverty, and harsh treatment of the poor, and the bitterness of His enemies, who at that moment were plotting to rid themselves of Him. Anyone else would have preached a condemning sermon against these abuses. At best they would have pleaded with the multitude, as the Apostle did, to share the burdens of their fellowmen. Jowett was right when he said, "God does not comfort us to make us comfortable, but to make us comforters." Although Jesus had that in mind long before He called the stumbling, weary multitude to His side, on this occasion He had something more to offer. Forgetting His own needs, He sought to bestow rest and comfort upon all who with unshaken faith and confidence would accept.

As we study the first three words, "Come unto me," we become aware He was not talking of a physical approach. He did not have to call those who were standing before Him. Rather was this an invitation to all people of all times. That which He would do for His audience He can still do for us. Coming to Jesus involves more than approach. Multitudes approached Him in His day. They recognized Him as the most astounding man ever to visit God's people. But many only came to see Him, to watch Him perform miracles, to listen to His words, and then depart. The only men He could depend upon were His disciples. The sightseers were as fickle as their followers have always been. They walked with Him one day, the next they were the followers of the world.

He had more than mere physical approach in mind when He spoke these words. He wanted individuals to share His spirit and that is a different matter. We cannot share the spirit of Christ without becoming like Him; thinking as He thought on the great issues of life; doing what God requires of His children. He also wanted them to bring Him all they had, their time, talents, and enthusiasm, that they might be used for a higher purpose. Coming to Jesus not only involves accepting His invitation but accepting Him. This has always been life's greatest choice. That is the approach Jesus desired. Is there not a challenge in that even for youth?

These words are for every person whose life is overloaded, and the causes of overloading are numerous. For many it is the tremendous burden of anxiety. Perhaps that includes us. If so, He calls us to come to Him and find rest. "People know you live in the realm of anxious care by the lines on your face, the tone of your voice, the minor key of your life, and the lack of joy

WHAT CHRIST WOULD DO FOR US

in your spirit. Scale the heights of a life abandoned to God, then you will look down on the clouds beneath your feet," said Darlow Sargeant. "And indeed you will," insisted Jesus. And it is for that reason He calls us unto Him.

There are many causes of anxiety. It may be the condition of some loved one. If we are not anxious about them now, the day will come when we will be. That loved one for many is a child. We are all concerned about those whom God has given us to protect, and what agonizing moments we spend while watching by their bedside! God would not expect us to look upon them without sharing their pain. They have all of our love, and the greatest feelings within man follow his love. If we do not possess great affections, we will experience no great sorrows. The stronger our love, the deeper the pain that comes with watching them feverishly tossing on their bed of sickness, and greater the tragedy if death intervenes. In that hour we need rest, the kind the Master can bestow by way of an inner calm and assurance. Perhaps it is not a baby, but the condition of a mother or father, husband or wife, brother or sister. In every case our needs are the same and Jesus has the answer for each need.

Maybe we are anxious about the future. God planned well when He made it impossible for us to see around the corner. Some of us might not be here today if we had known what awaited us. It was the hope within that kept us going. Without it we would have been lost, and our strength sapped when the crisis came. Tomorrow might not treat us kindly, for it has a way of being harsh as well as kind. But God is in tomorrow whatever comes, and so is Christ. They offer us rest — rest from our anxious fears, and they are stronger than anything tomorrow can bring. The words by Laura A. Barter Snow sing of the blessings in our unknown tomorrows because of God's presence.

> God is in every tomorrow,
>   Therefore I live for today,
> Certain of finding at sunrise,
>   Guidance and strength for the way;
> Power for each moment of weakness,
>   Hope for each moment of pain,
> Comfort for every sorrow,
>   Sunshine and joy after rain.

Many are anxious because of their own bodily weakness. How distraught we become when suspecting something wrong! I was in conversation a few weeks ago with a man who confessed that fear kept him from a much needed operation. A question mark appeared after the results and he continues through the days with that anxious load upon his mind. Tragic? Yes, but there are thousands like him. It is no trivial matter. They need our love and encouragement, but they need Jesus, too, and the rest He offers.

Perhaps our anxiety is due to soul-weariness. We are not happy spiritually. Many are off balance. The weariness of the soul can be more distressing than weariness of the body. The prevailing causes of soul-weariness are many. The consciousness of our sin is, of course, the greatest. We can never be happy while doing that we know to be wrong. Every day the newspapers tell of men, women, and young people who can

WHAT CHRIST WOULD DO FOR US

no longer stand the strain of riotous living. Their collapse is complete, but only a few have come to the place where to them life is unbearable. The vast majority live unhappy lives, either unmindful, or not caring, that what they need is Jesus and the spiritual rest He can give.

Temptation is a prevalent source of soul-weariness. To those who have tried to break some vicious habit, temptation is always present. I still remember the testimony of a man given years before I entered the ministry. The story of his salvation parallels many running through the course of Christian history. The greatest temptation following his conversion was drink. He fought it night and day. Whenever he passed a saloon the odor was sufficient to revive his former desires, yet he kept manfully on. One hot summer day, while suffering from thirst and an apparently lowered moral resistance, he attempted to pass the many saloons which at that time dotted the streets of Boston's South End. He passed several but seemed powerless to move beyond the next. On one corner of the street stood the place he used to frequent in the days before his conversion. On the other was a drug store. He started for the saloon door, but just as he was to enter he remembered his promise. Immediately changing his course he ran to the drug store, entered a telephone booth, took down the receiver and cried in the mouthpiece, "O God, if you have ever helped anyone, help me now!" Help, he said, did come. His shivering body soon began to quiet. His thirst had disappeared. He left the drug store and walked by the saloon a conqueror.

LIFE BEGINS WITH JESUS

Our doubts and hours of testing always cause soul-weariness. If you have been troubled with doubts you will understand what I am about to say. When I dedicated my life to the ministry, I did it by way of an altar service. It seemed impossible that my faith would ever wane. However, when I entered theological school, I found that much I believed was out of harmony with modern thought. I had to unlearn a great deal, and the process raised innumerable questions in my mind. Later, I became pastor of a little church in New Hampshire. For nearly a year the struggle continued. I was not happy. With doubts that almost overwhelmed me I sought to bring messages of faith to my people. Finally, the victory was won, but only after wrestling long and earnestly in prayer. I found rest in Jesus and never in the intervening years has my faith been shaken. I am thankful now for that period, for it prepared me for the suffering and sorrow that followed.

We are overloaded with many things. Whatever they are it is a sign we need Jesus. We might not be conscious of His presence, but He is always near. E. H. Divall tells of his nearness by way of poetry.

> He is not far away:
> Why do we sometimes seem to be alone,
> And miss the hands outstretched to meet our own?
> He is the same today
>
> As when of old He dwelt
> In human form with His disciples — when
> He knew the needs of all His fellowmen,
> And all their sorrows felt.

WHAT CHRIST WOULD DO FOR US

> Only our faith is dim,
> So that our eyes are holden, and we go
> All day, and until dusk, before we know
> That we have walked with Him.

The Master has much to offer, but rest is a necessity. It places us beside Him and guidance is assured. Temptation will still face us. It did Jesus. It is recorded that after the victory on the Mount of Temptation, Satan left Him for a season. He faced temptation after that and so will we, but the rest He gives equips and provides us with strength to conquer. We will be tempted, but we will have His strength as well as ours, and that provides power to overcome. "The strength of the vessel can be demonstrated only by the hurricane," said William Taylor, "and the power of the Gospel can be fully shown only when the Christian is subject to some fiery trial."

Suffering will be before us. The Son of Man was never free from it. The final chapter of His life before the resurrection was cruel and painful. And whether we are in Christ or not, pain and suffering will visit us. But His rest prepares us for it, and when it comes we can meet it triumphantly, for we face it with Him. Neither can sorrow be escaped. The victorious Christ stopped in the midst of His triumphal procession to weep in sorrow over the sins of Jerusalem. To accept this invitation is no guarantee that we will escape anything experienced by others. The same strength offered them is likewise extended to us. It is the acceptance or rejection of this that makes the difference. It comes as suggested in the verse by Julius Sturm:

LIFE BEGINS WITH JESUS

> Pain's furnace heat within me quivers;
>   God's breath upon the flame doth blow.
> And all my heart in anguish shivers,
>   And trembles at the fiery glow;
> And yet I whisper, "As God will!"
> And in the hottest fire hold still.

What is the rest He offers? There are those who would reply the rest needed is the cessation of everything that tires. Complete relaxation, stretched out in the shade without a care or worry. Forgotten are the painful hours of labor. Forgotten, too, the burdens that have pressed so heavily upon us. Just rest at the feet of the Master. A lazy man's dream, the tramp's idea of paradise. But is that what Jesus desires to give? One glance at the disciples will provide the answer. They were constantly with Him. Surely they must have had an abundance of this rest that He offered the multitude. Yet how many times do we find them sitting lazily around? As we read the Gospels, we become aware that Jesus kept them always on the move. Following the days of Pentecost, idle moments were unknown. Although they had accepted this invitation, we now find them ministering night and day, being hunted, persecuted, mobbed, and murdered. It appears, then, that the rest Jesus intended to bestow is different than that ordinarily expected.

Of course He recognized the value of physical relaxation. He rested and insisted that His disciples do likewise. But this invitation was different. It was not the spirit of repose but rest in the midst of turmoil. Work we must do. It was not His spirit to encourage

WHAT CHRIST WOULD DO FOR US

laziness. He knew that this was the source of weariness. There is nothing as boring as an empty life. He was continually calling people to do something, and His demands were always hard — far harder than that which the most active and alert wanted to undertake. But in Him rest can be found in the midst of the most exacting toil. That is more in keeping with the spirit of God and the life of the Master than a shiftless, indolent existence.

It was rest from degrading bondage that He underlined. He told the story of a young man who had become of age, and decided it was time to leave home. He had no intentions of destroying the finer things of his life when he gathered his possessions to depart. No young man does. His greatest wonder was why his father should be so concerned. How foolish! How old-fashioned! Fathers must be made of peculiar material, he reasoned, as he left to see the world, to taste life and do the things he dreamed of, free from parental restraints. But that which he didn't expect soon took place. The rest he thought would be his was exceedingly rare and fleeting. The freedom he longed for, he lost. He became a slave, living and eating with swine. Jesus, however, refused to let the story end there. He pictured two yearning hearts. The young man, when he came to himself, yearned for the fellowship of his father. He no longer considered him as queer. He understood now, as he recalled sadly what his father meant to him. He yearned for home, the place he was so anxious to leave. He desired forgiveness and rest. None of these were found in his place of bondage. And when he left the squalid confines of his prison, he learned that his father, who had yearned for him, was not content to remain indoors until he knocked and sought forgiveness, but when he was yet afar off he saw him, ran, put his arms around him, and kissed him. Rest came only after he had cast aside his chains and returned to his father's house. And that is the rest Jesus offers to all who still remain in the far country, shackled to their sins. "God only knows how blessed He could make us if we would let Him," said George MacDonald. "And that," says Jesus, "is what I desire to do."

The Master has infinitely more to offer us than we have to give Him. Yet all He asks is for the gift of ourselves. He is not concerned with how much more it will cost Him. He would be terribly concerned if we refused this invitation.

WHY LEAVE JESUS?
"From that time many of his disciples went back, and walked no more with him." — JOHN 6:66

IT IS strange that some people leave Jesus at the moment their need of Him is greatest. This is not always easy to understand. We would not leave a skilled surgeon when informed that only by way of an operation could our lives be saved. We would not leave our place of employ when informed of a long awaited promotion. The survivors of a torpedoed vessel would not refuse rescue or the weary a chance to gain a well deserved rest. Yet in the hour when Christ is needed most, many depart and walk with Him no more.

"From that time," says our text, "many of his disciples went back and walked no more with him." What time was that? It was the time He tried to convey to them His mission. He had come to save His people from their sins, and that was what these followers needed—a Saviour. They had looked forward to the coming of God's Son, and here He was now in their midst, but they didn't like what He said.

It was the time when He declared He was the bread of life. They were anxious for bread. In fact they asked for it, but the bread they sought was of the variety that lasted only one meal. A few hours later they would be as hungry as now. If He continued to feed them, they would continue to follow. However, the bread He offered was Himself. They would never hunger if they fed on Him, and Jesus knew how famished their souls were. This was the bread they lacked, yet they left that for the food so easily provided.

LIFE BEGINS WITH JESUS

It was the time He revealed the unescapable cross looming directly in the path ahead, and warned that to be His followers would mean facing it too. We can understand some things about human nature, but hardly how anyone can leave Jesus when facing a cross.

As this sermon began to take shape, I tried to think back over my ministry and count the many who had left Him in the hour a cross appeared. Some of the experiences I knew; others were unfolded as I visited the homes of my parishioners. It is true the number is not large, but they represent a sad, despondent, disillusioned company that are to be found in every community as well as every nation of the world.

For some it was the hour of material loss. With their earthly possessions went their faith. "Little minds," said Washington Irving, "are tamed and subdued by misfortune, but great minds rise above it." Christians should not be defeated by the unexpected. When that happens they lose more than the treasures that through the years have been clutched in greedy hands. What a time to lose faith! That was when they needed Jesus, yet it marked the turning point for it was then they walked with Him no more.

For many it was a season of long suffering ending in a physical handicap. Surely they could not do without Him then, yet they departed from His presence, and through the years found nothing to help them in their trouble.

For others it was a great sorrow. Leave Christ in such an hour as that! Lose Him, too! That is leaving the only hope we have. David Hume not only ques-

WHY LEAVE JESUS?

tioned things divine and aired his doubts openly, but he persuaded his aged mother to give up her faith in God. In the midst of sorrow, with hopes dashed and unable to find comfort in her unbelief, she turned pathetically to the cause of her distress, and said, "My son, you have taken away my religion; now tell me something to help comfort me." He could not, for he had nothing to relieve the pain and remorse that suddenly overwhelmed him. That is the moment Jesus offers the greatest hope. We not only receive comfort and consolation from His words, but the assurance that only through Him will we be united with our loved ones. To leave Him is to leave our only source of light and life, and these disciples left Jesus at the time when He was indispensable — when they faced a cross.

It was also the time when death was suggested. His death, to be sure, but they were to follow Him even to that. People may leave Christ when the sunshine of buoyant health beats down upon them, and unfortunately too many do. But sunshine has a way of fading, often without notice. That happens when one is facing the morning or noon of life, but to leave Christ when the shadows reveal the fast approaching night is beyond understanding. Our experience has been that the most sinful make every effort to find Him when the night of death settles in. But these followers listened as the Master Himself revealed that coming hour, yet went back to their old ways of living. "When all is prosperous, we talk about God," said Oliver Huckel. "When death draws nigh, we talk to Him."

Why do people leave Jesus? We know many of the

prevailing answers, but our Scripture provides information that is as true today as when the incident occurred.

In the first place, these disciples soon came to the conclusion that following Jesus was not easy. They turned back after He had said something that caused them to murmur and complain that it was a hard saying. It was the easy they wanted, not the hard. They didn't relish being disturbed, yet how unreasonable. They faced the hard every day, but did not turn from it. Life was hard. It is for every person born into this world, but they did not flee from that. They went on living and took the difficult knowing it could not be avoided. Their work was hard. Most of them were toilers. Some were workers in the field; others were fishermen. The women in their group bore their share of hardness without outward complaint. The gaining of an education was not easy. We do not know who composed this group, but Jesus had contact with well-trained men throughout His ministry. There is no reason to think that only the unschooled followed Him.

There are many who leave Jesus for the same reason today. We learn after a time that His is not a leisurely road and that disturbs us. We want Him to say smooth things, leaving out that which would upset us and our plans. We want Him to please us, but He did not come to entertain but to save, and that is different. That requires much from us as well as from Him. We want Him, yet in such a way that we can go on living as though He did not exist. We protest that this is not the case. We love Him, we say, and are terribly of-

WHY LEAVE JESUS?

fended when our devotion is questioned. Lustily we sing, "My Jesus I love Thee, I know Thou art mine," yet we take Him so lightly. How slow we are to arise at His command and follow Him! With what ease we push Him aside when we desire to please ourselves! It is hard for men to relinquish their greed, intolerance, immoral practices, injustice, and intemperance, and when it is discovered that His teachings condemn this, many turn and walk no more with Him. Although His love for us is always consistant, our repeated infatuations for that which is out of harmony with His life is a commentary on human fickleness.

In the second place, many of these disciples followed Jesus because they sought worldly security. That is a human trait, a very natural thing to expect. They had followed Him over a road made comparatively easy, but now that road was beginning to go uphill. The dream of a worldly kingdom, with its splendor, wealth, and a life of ease, was appealing. Not that Christ had offered such, but many who had walked with Him felt that this was the ultimate goal, and when judged from a material point of view they had grounds for their false hopes. They had witnessed His power, and beheld the results of His miracles. Surely He could give everything man desired. They were living in a real world, and they craved that which would make their present life complete.

There are few hours when the mind of man is not centered upon the life He now lives. He must have food, clothing, and shelter. He desires health and hopes for years of prosperity. All this seemed possible

LIFE BEGINS WITH JESUS

through the efforts of the amazing young Preacher, whose power appeared unlimited. It is true they did not grasp all that He had said, but that mattered little if He could bring about the fulfillment of their dreams. But He had sensed their feelings too. He knew what was in man. Even His own disciples shared many of the prevailing views. This could not go on and Jesus must make it understood. Thus of late He had been talking about the possibilities of suffering. The idea of a cross began to appear upon the horizon. This was rugged climbing for those who sought Him for worldly security only, so they decided it was not worth the effort. "You cannot fight the French with two hundred thousand red uniforms," stormed Carlyle, "there must be men inside of them." When men who lack courage are inside the uniform, when the going is hard, retreat is the order of the day. We are not surprised, therefore, to read, " many of his disciples went back and walked no more with him."

These are hard, cruel words. It is a tragic moment when friends desert. It is even more tragic at the time a cross looms, and the pathway ahead is filled with sorrow. But perhaps it is not as tragic as it seems. A sifting process is always beneficial and the time for it is before the shadows deepen. It is better for a desertion to take place before the storm than in the midst of it. It might be disconcerting now, but it would be heart-breaking then. Jesus knew that those who remained would at least be more loyal and dependable. However, His own disciples showed signs of wavering, and He asked, "Will ye also go away?" Whether or

WHY LEAVE JESUS?

not they were prepared to answer "No," we can only surmise. Perhaps Peter didn't give them a chance, but his words overshadowed anything the others could say, and to them they unanimously gave their approval.

In the third place, there were some in this group for whom Jesus had become an old story. For many it doesn't take long for the familiar to grow stale. We have all witnessed the rise and fall of leaders in every walk of life, not that they necessarily have changed, but because of man's nature many grow tired of the same face, the same voice, the same leader. There were some among the group recorded in our Scripture who left the Master because to them He had become a familiar figure.

It would be well for us to sit alone in some quiet place and think of what would happen if the familiar should suddenly be taken from us. How familiar the sunshine, rain, and quietness of night are? Jesus, the Bible, the church, the Sabbath Day are considered of no immediate importance to many. Our homes and loved ones are not sufficiently appreciated. But what if these should be removed?

Jesus, too, has become so familiar that multitudes who call themselves Christians no longer walk with Him. Even in the short space of His ministry He ceased to be interesting to many that He once thrilled. This is only to be expected, for men have always spurned those who would save them, scathingly ridiculed the best, and departed from all with whom they have failed to agree or made no attempt to understand. Even one of His disciples left. Not now, but in the most crucial hour. Maybe Judas was the one who looked a little too longingly at the departure of the other disciples on this occasion. If such were the case it would have been better if the Master had let him go.

But back to our place of quiet again. The result of our meditation has been that with the passing of the familiar, life would go, too. Face the world tomorrow! What kind of a world would it be? Barren, cold, wicked, cruel, and friendless. Peter must have realized this when he said, "Lord, to whom shall we go?"

In the fourth place, there were some in this group who walked no more with Jesus because of the sudden awareness that He was an extremist. He was unorthodox. Whom should they love? Their friends, of course. Yet Jesus had told them to love their enemies. Whom should they respect? The answer would be, men of wealth. They were the outstanding of their community. The men to whom they bowed. Even the village in which I lived as a boy felt that. Women bowed, children looked in awe, and men spoke in almost reverent tones to the one man of wealth. And these people of the Master's day looked with respect upon the wealthy who kept them in continual servitude. Yet they had heard this young preacher say, "It is easier for a camel to go through the eye of a needle, than for a rich man to enter into the kingdom of God."

Whom should they despise? The publicans and sinners. But these were the ones Jesus sought. He

WHY LEAVE JESUS?

had already been accused of eating with them. He even called one such to be His disciple, and when Matthew accepted, he prepared a banquet, inviting his publican friends to dine with him, and Jesus was in the midst of these outcasts. This tendency of the Master was not only obnoxious to the loyal Jew, but unforgivable.

Who were the heroes? Bold warriors, mighty conquerors, but Jesus did not include them in His list of the outstanding. Instead He had said, "Blessed are the peacemakers; for they shall be called the children of God." Who were the greatest? Were they not the rulers? But when Jesus had spoken of greatness He talked in terms of a childlike spirit.

Where was life to be found? How was it to be gained? These disciples knew the accepted answer, but now as they listened to Him He said, "I am the bread of life." Life was to be found by feeding on Him. At this they departed for He was too radical for them. And for the same reasons many forsake Him today. "You can't apply His words," is the cry, and, consequently, His words are not applied. Hold up, if you will, Christianity and war, and see how distinctly opposed to each other they are. War could not happen if the teachings of Jesus were followed, but He is considered an extremist and war continues. Place business and the teachings of Christ side by side and you will notice that they are still far apart. We have always heard that business and religion will not mix, but what is being substituted for His words concerning the subject? Compare His teachings and the prevailing view of life and you will notice how distinctly different they are. The world is not right. Life is being interpreted on a plane far too low and the results are disasterous.

Finally, many left Him because they demanded action and He gave only words. "Feed us," they urged, and He said, "I am the bread of life feed on me." Even Peter caught the thought of the crowd. Perhaps he heard someone ridiculing the Master for His words. But Peter knew that what Jesus said was not the ordinary sayings of men, and he cried: "Thou hast the words of eternal life."

Today men desert Him because they demand action, not words. "What is Christ doing?" they ask, then answer their own question with, "Nothing." In a world at war, in the midst of turmoil and suffering, where is Christ? Why isn't He doing something? And the deserters answer, "Don't you know? He is only speaking. Words, words, but no action." Sidney Smith once said, "Never try to reason the prejudice out of man. It was not reasoned into him and cannot be reasoned out."

How blind we are! How little we know concerning the power of words! What transformed a pagan world? What is behind every activity that leads towards the redemption of men? Life? Yes, but that life would not be complete apart from the words that inspired His followers to advance His cause no matter what the cost. By way of these words men have been saved, hope has flashed upon darkened horizons, pain, suffering, sorrow have been overcome

WHY LEAVE JESUS?

and turned into channels of blessing. This is another way of saying that the greatest activity the world has ever witnessed has come as a result of the words of Christ. The words of eternal life mean action. He was the Word.

These are some of the reasons why Christ was deserted. The demand is much the same now as in the days of His ministry. We are so slow to understand! We want a Saviour patterned after a wordly conqueror. We still revel in show and pomp. That which He once refused to do we insist is the only way for His Kingdom to advance. Therefore we leave Him. But to whom shall we go? Surely the deserters have not chosen a higher road. Until a better way is suggested or a better man appears we shall continue to follow Him. Nearly two thousand years have not produced His equal. A million years will not, for He has no equal. Let us then take heart, follow Him more closely, and we will yet see revealed everything He promised.

A PEEP INTO HEAVEN

"In my Father's house are many mansions   I go to prepare a place for you." — JOHN 14:2

THESE ARE among the most beloved words ever spoken. Jesus left the best for the last. We are familiar with the vibrant messages given in the upper room. In them are to be found the most precious promises of the Christian faith, yet how simple they are! When we attempt to speak of life everlasting we speculate, condemn certain prevailing views, present arguments to support our own, and when completed we have given a scholarly dissertation. Jesus used simple language and made it so appealing and inviting that it challenges us. When these words were spoken He was not reminding the disciples of what others thought or even what He considered likely. It was based not upon theory but upon fact. He knew, and therefore revealed what had hitherto been hidden. And His own composure tends to bear out the confidence He had in the future as well as accurate knowledge concerning it.

We commonly speak of this last night as the final chapter of His life. To Jesus it was only the beginning, and He was informing the disciples of what was ahead as one would describe some home he was about to occupy and of which he knew every nook and corner. "In My Father's House," He says, "are many mansions: if it were not so, I would have told you. I go to prepare a place for you." The disciples might question that home but not the Master. They might speak of the future as they had the out-of-doors that night, the darkness beyond their lighted room. Jesus spoke of it as He did the familiar objects within the light of the room.

It is strange how guarded we are in what we say, especially when viewed in the light of assurance given by Jesus. There are some who would not want to raise false hopes. Jesus reminds us that our hopes will be false if we do not vision the future as He did. He was not walking over an unknown road. He knew every step of it. It does not grow darker as one moves ever away from the light of this world, but as He proceeds we become conscious that the road grows brighter. The darkness, in reality, is the puny little light we know in this world and always thought to be so bright.

In the first place, Jesus describes Heaven in terms not only familiar but dear to the human heart. The thought of it being the Father's House is enticing. That is where we are ushered when the lights are extinguished here. Someone remarked not long ago, "The grave is the end." Apparently they were unfamiliar with this thrilling message. Jesus never mentioned the grave, but His Father's House. I think we need to learn this if we have not already done so. I have a friend who visits the grave of his wife every day, and when he leaves bids her good-bye. He is sincerely in earnest, but very much mistaken. His wife is not there but in the Father's House. We know the Master understands and feels even more keenly for him than do his friends. It is a splendid thing to

A PEEP INTO HEAVEN

still visit with, and talk to, his loved one, but he can do it far more effectively in his own home.

When Jesus finished it seemed as though the Father's House was so near one could reach it by a few steps. We think of it in terms of distance. The writer of Hebrews speaks of being "compassed about with so great a cloud of witnesses," and we hardly understand. It is because our distance is all out of proportion. Our loved ones are near, nearer than we dare think. We would be amazed if the curtain should suddenly be removed and we caught a glimpse of that which appears so vague and remote.

For Jesus it was likewise a familiar place. He always lived in it. That is the reason for the confidence He engendered when He talked about it. It should be a familiar place to us. Even though we might not possess the inside knowledge He had, we have His word and should not that be sufficient?

We notice also the emphasis He placed upon the word "father." Jesus always spoke of God as a father, and because Heaven is the Father's House we are surely not afraid to enter. Neither have we come to the place where we have outgrown the need of a father's loving ministry. "Father!" sneered Heine. "We are of age, and do not need a father's care." That is what another man thought, of whom the Bible says, "The fool hath said in his heart, There is no God."

There is nothing in the word "father" to frighten us. This makes God real and His House inviting. Sometimes we refer to Him as Creator, but we know

LIFE BEGINS WITH JESUS

very little about that office. It develops a distance too great for us to bridge. But when we think of Him as Father we understand.

I have a father who means much to me. From him I have learned something about fatherhood. I have been given the privilege of being a father, and know something about that responsibility. No matter what else we understand about God, when Jesus speaks of Him as Father we catch a new vision. It provides a common bond between us. To step into Heaven is to enter the presence of the greatest father of all. "After all," remarked Dr. Rainy, near the close of his life, "immortality is a dreary prospect if our Father is not in it." Of course it is. The motherhood of God is as real as His fatherhood, and Heaven without Him would be equivalent to a home without parents.

The first word Joanne ever uttered was "Daddy." As she grew older the word did not change but the meaning did. It meant protection. She was never frightened when in my arms. I realized my limitations, but she did not. The presence of her daddy assured her of safety. The boy and girl growing into life, having passed through more years than my little four-year-old, still feel the need of leaning upon their father. The young person goes to him for guidance. God is like that and more. When we become weak, His strong arms support us. When we lose our way in the gloom of doubts and skepticism, He becomes a light unto our path. When we stumble over the many protruding obstacles, He in His infinite mercy strength-

A PEEP INTO HEAVEN

ens us and enables us to stand. When death enters our home, He lifts the burden that would otherwise crush our already wounded heart and gives us comfort. When we are discouraged and broken in spirit He speaks to us through His Son saying, "Let not your heart be troubled, neither let it be afraid." When sin has overwhelmed us and we cry aloud for mercy, His answer is cast in the same mold of love, "Though your sins be as scarlet, they shall be as white as snow."

It was not only the fatherhood of God that Jesus stressed but the Father's House. That means home, and home is the dearest place we know. God planned well when He placed in our heart the desire to be homemakers. Perhaps He was preparing us for that other home yet unseen. We do not shrink from the thought, but rejoice in the fact that the place we love here — home — will not be denied, when, for the last time, we lock the doors of our earthly house and move to one not made by human hands.

Home is where we know each other. It could not be that apart from recognition. Home is the center of love, and love produces harmony, happiness, and peace. We enjoy being where these reside. It is the seat of genuine understanding. And as such is a refuge, a sanctuary, a haven. It is a shelter from the world.

A home is the storehouse of many of our earthly treasures. To be sure, they would not bring much in the open market, but are priceless to us. They carry a price tag mercenary hands cannot affix. Those who made them, who have carefully preserved them through the years, or fondly looked upon them as choice possessions, have moved to another home. In their lives rests the value that turns common household articles into treasures.

An auction disposing of the furnishings of an old homestead is a tragic spectacle. An auctioneer, with clumsy, irreverent hands, mauls everything in sight. Buyers looking for bargains hotly bid for the furnishings they want, disdainfully rejecting that which appears without value. What no one can see is that through the years that old homestead has stored up something money cannot buy. How many tears have fallen from weary, fearful eyes, as someone knelt upon the carpet in sincere prayer for a loved one, that carpet now being thrown in the arms of the highest bidder! How many nights have loving hands ministered to the sick, tossing feverishly upon the beds of that home, or a mother sat in the worn-out rocking chair, holding to her bosom the dear little babe weakened by disease!

There are treasures in a home that cannot be bought at any price. Love, faith, joy, sorrow, tears, suffering, loving ministry — these are but a few of the unpurchasables. Heaven is a home, and the treasures no purchaser can buy are stored there. Let us not think for one moment that the real values of the old homestead remain within its walls. They are stored up above "where neither moth nor rust doth corrupt, and where thieves do not break through nor steal." As I turn my eyes in that direction I realize how wealthy I am, and the vastness of it overwhelms me. I not only have the

A PEEP INTO HEAVEN

Master and the assurance of life everlasting, but my wife is there. What treasures for a man to gaze upon!

> My heart is there!
> Where? On eternal hills, my loved one dwells
> Among the lilies and asphodels,
> Clad in the brightness of the Great White Throne.
> Glad in the smile of Him who sits thereon,
> The glory gilding all His wealth of hair
> And making His immortal face more fair —
> There is my treasure and my heart is there.

In the second place, He indicates the preparation He is to make. "I go to prepare a place for you." Someone remarked recently that we prepare our own heaven. To a certain extent this may be true, for I know what the speaker meant, but this isn't what Jesus said. He realized our prepared heaven might satisfy us, whose minds were centered around earthly things, but it would not fit into the greater plans of God. Let us be thankful it is Jesus who does the preparing, for that will afford the greatest surprise our eyes can behold.

Have you ever considered what poor builders we are? It seems certain we would not be oversuccessful in preparing a Heaven. Even the best of us will be stunned when we view what the Master has prepared.

We cannot help but notice the emphasis Jesus placed on the word "you." "It is expedient for you," He said, "that I go away." His concern was not for Himself, but for us. He loved His disciples so deeply that it was their welfare He was considering, and speaking of His impending departure He again reminds them, "I go to prepare a place for you." He was not compelled to go, but went freely. The cross would bring suffering. The hours preceding would cause pain. The injustice of those whom He was anxious to save would break His heart. But that seemed minor when compared to all He wanted to do for His own.

We have all had the experience of preparing for someone. Elaborate plans are made. We fix things just so, and even though that preparation would require doing many things the same for all our friends, there would nevertheless be a little extra touch for each one. We know them so well that we would not consider our work complete until the little extras were added. "And that," reminds Jesus, "is what I am doing."

There is another side that we cannot overlook. It is seen from our angle. The greatest preparation in a home is, after all, the person we are going to see. It would make little difference how well a home had been cleaned and polished if the person we yearn for should not be present when we arrive. We would be greatly disappointed. That home, however artistically arranged, would be a lonely, desolate place. The presence of Jesus is the greatest preparation for that home beyond. To be with Him, and enjoy His fellowship, would be enough.

To prepare a place for one signifies we expect them, and when they arrive we are on hand with warm, friendly greetings. When Jesus prepares a place for us He expects us. We will not arrive unexpectedly.

A PEEP INTO HEAVEN

It will not come as a surprise. He will be there to greet us. It always is a tragedy when our loved ones go while still young, yet we know their place is ready.

Another thought is essential, that although the Master prepares a place for us, we must prepare ourselves for that place. We know that in this He has been disappointed, for many a prepared place has not been occupied. The thought my friend had in mind, and which is most essential, is to so live that we may become the best possible occupants of the place reserved for us.

In the third place, He discloses that His departure is not final. "I will come again," He says. We are amazed at His thoughtfulness. "I go for you. I will come again." Our scholars remind us that this should read, "I come again," and the "will" was included through faulty translation. This does seem to be more in keeping with His spirit. His coming is continuous in all our varied experiences. He comes in our loneliness, despondency, pain, and sorrow. He also comes prodding our conscience during hours of sunshine when the tendency is to forget Him. He even comes in our sin. "Behold I stand at the door and knock." And the purpose for His coming is always that He might receive us unto Himself. He does not want to lose one disciple. Every person is precious in His sight and He desires to receive us unto Himself now that we may be His forever. That is the reason for His yearning, His patient seeking, His refusal to give up in despair of any soul, no matter how seemingly impossible or unworthy they may appear.

LIFE BEGINS WITH JESUS

The coming of Jesus is not confined to life's varied experiences. He comes not merely unto us, but for us, in that experience we call death. Are we afraid of death? Do we consider it as an ominous shadow that looms somewhere ahead in our pathway? If we do, let us remember that for the Christian, death is Jesus coming for His own. Many who know the tender care received by loving hands in their physical weakness, and possess implicit faith in the ability of their doctor, face their sufferings unafraid. But when the thought of death presents itself, refusing to be banished, they cry for loving hands as though they never again would feel them. May we rest assured that the most loving arms of all will be around us in that hour, for it is then Jesus receives us unto Himself. When that moment arrives, we will hear His voice assuring us, "It is I, be not afraid." Nathaniel Hawthorne has written:

> When death is at hand, and the cottage of clay
> Is left with a tremulous sigh,
> The Gracious Forerunner is smoothing the way
> For its tenant to pass to unchangeable day,
> Saying, "Be not afraid, it is I."
>
> When the waters are passed, and the glories unknown
> Burst forth on the wondering eye,
> The compassionate "Lamb in the midst of the throne"
> Shall welcome, encourage, and comfort His own,
> And say, "Be not afraid, it is I."

We do not enter the pathway of death alone. We are met at the door by the Great Physician, but He is not the only one to meet us. Our loved ones will be there to greet us also.

A PEEP INTO HEAVEN

On our island we have the habit of meeting the boat. My wife particularly enjoyed doing this especially when someone was coming to visit us. I remember how eagerly she watched, and the expression of joy that came over her face when she saw those for whom she was looking, and she was usually the first to see them. Do you suppose that this desire has left her or her sight in any way diminished? In that day when you, whom she knew and loved, shall leave on the last boat for that destination, she will be on hand to greet you. Your loved ones will be there, too. You will not sail alone, for Jesus will be with you. You will not arrive among strangers. Death is not the cruel thing the world presents it to be. As we were received by loving arms and every possible attention when we came into this world, we may be sure our reception will be even more elaborate when we leave.

Finally, He presents His reason for this extensive preparation. "Where I am, there ye may be also." There are times when we look back wistfully to the day in which He lived and feel that we have missed much because we did not have the opportunity of seeing Him and listening to His words. Perhaps one reason many are impatient for His return is that they might see Him and follow Him. However, He has made ample provision for our yearning in this direction. No disciple will ever miss this opportunity. We cannot go back two thousand years. He has not come in visible form, yet we can press to our hearts the happy thought that this desired fellowship will be ours. We can be with Him here and have that companionship now. But there is reserved for us the glad surprise of seeing Him as He is, listening to His voice, and remaining in His presence always, and to be with Him is to be with all the saints.

Let us take heart and rejoice! We have a hope, not devised by man, but by God. We have a Saviour who is alive forevermore. We weep when our loved ones depart and we have every reason to. God gave us that love and He does not expect us to treat it lightly or brush it aside. We weep when the shadows of this life close around us, not for ourselves but those left behind. They are still our concern. And in this, too, God would not have it otherwise. Therefore He has provided the greatest reason for rejoicing in the midst of our tears by giving Jesus, whose presence meant life to those who touched Him in Galilee, and who prepares a place for us, that where He is there we may be also.

PAUL'S CLEVEREST SAYING

"Now if any man have not the Spirit of Christ, he is none of his." — ROMANS 8:9

THE WORDS of Paul have been the subject of debate and research of scholars of all ages. He was profound, yet so simple; scholarly, yet so much like the rest of humanity. He was not only profound, he was clever, and clever sayings always appeal. The above text is a combination of both. These words are profound in their simplicity. They are a constant reminder that life begins with Jesus. That was always the message of the great Apostle. It is the only message consistent with Christian living.

Who is a Christian? How can we tell? How can we be sure? Is he one who can recite every outstanding verse of the Bible? Perhaps so, but we have learned through painful experience that not every pious, Scripture quoting Christian possessed the spirit of Christ. A good memory can retain precious promises, but good memories are not always associated with good lives.

Can we judge a Christian by his church affiliation? A certain portion of the church would answer in the affirmative. Outside of their faith there can be no salvation. Yet Christ went so far as to say, "Other sheep I have, which are not of this fold." He didn't count His followers in terms of any group. This is not the final test of the Christian life. Some day we will learn that pious souls are distributed quite evenly throughout the church. The test of a Christian goes beyond the portals of the church he attends.

LIFE BEGINS WITH JESUS

Is a Christian determined by his mode of worship? Is it all summed up in the way he was baptized or the method by which he takes communion? There are many who will not take communion from any other hands than an ordained minister of their denomination, and the mode of baptism has all too often become a dividing wedge instead of a uniting bond.

Is a Christian determined solely by his labor of love? The church has no appeal for an untold number who are willing to let their future rest on the good they do. "Inasmuch as ye have done it unto one of the least of these my brethren, ye have done it unto me," are the only words of the Master they seem to know.

Are these the tests we are to apply to the Christian life? Do they not leave us with a sense of uncertainty? We do not know; we are not sure.

These are not the final tests of the Christian life. They raise too many questions. They foster too many doubts. There is one test, however, that is final. There can be no question about it. It is the test of our text: the possession of the spirit of Christ. Whenever you meet a person who can qualify in this direction, forget his denomination, his mode of worship, and his social standing, for you have found a Christian. This is only to be expected, for no one can possess the spirit of Christ without being like Him. No wonder Paul was so sure. The absence of that spirit automatically disqualifies one. The fact that he has a Christian name, grew up in a Christian home, is the citizen of a Christian nation, and calls himself a

PAUL'S CLEVEREST SAYING

Christian doesn't make him one. That which counts is the spirit of Christ.

In the first place, the spirit of Christ consists of an absolute trust and confidence in God. Jesus didn't always understand, but His faith was so great it made little difference. He simply talked it over as we would our problems with an earthly father. To the poor, distressed, bewildered, fearful souls of His day He said, "Take no anxious thought for your life, stop worrying about food, clothes, and shelter; let tomorrow take care of itself. Why? Because God knows all about you and your needs. Trust Him and He will care for you." These are not easy words for us to remember when we face the needs of tomorrow. Food, clothes, sickness, old age, death — are not these the number one worries of the world? They were in the Master's day, yet He so trusted God he lived above them, giving them no anxious thought. When we possess the spirit of Christ we will likewise go on living daily, trusting God to care for us.

Together with trust was His obedience. He always obeyed God. His ministry is a reflection of that obedience. It is never absent from His teaching. The cross gives emphasis to the distance He was willing to go.

Neither can we overlook His dependence upon God. He leaned upon Him for guidance. He would not have conquered in Gethsemane had He left the outcome to chance. His desire was to do His Father's will, and on this occasion it was that the cup should not pass from Him. Calvary must be faced.

LIFE BEGINS WITH JESUS

It is well for us to pause and look often at Gethsemane, we who cry out against God; who say He is unfair and unkind in His leadership; who feel that He is sometimes utterly cruel. After God's will had been made known, when there could be no mistake, Jesus did not lift His voice against Him. He did not go to the disciples fussing and grumbling, insisting that His Father was unfair. Instead, He immediately prepared Himself for the cross. He was satisfied that God knew best. He was the most composed and optimistic person in the upper room.

But guidance was only a part of His dependence. Coupled with it was strength. To be guided in difficult channels is one thing; to possess the necessary strength to go through is another. Jesus depended upon His Father for that. We do not have the spirit of Christ if our trust in, obedience to, and dependence upon God does not in some measure match His.

In the second place, the spirit of Christ is revealed in His attitude toward men. Notice His insistence to be of service. He didn't expect others to serve Him. He insisted that He came to minister, that was God's plan. It was His one great desire. It made no difference who the people were or the condition of their lives. He was at home when He sat by the well-side preaching to a sinful woman, or at dinner with a despised tax collector. These were opportunities for service. A scholar came to Him by night, a rich young man by day, and He had a message for each. He ministered to all who had some need, and He taught by way of His life as well

PAUL'S CLEVEREST SAYING

as His words. "Learn of me," He said, and His life of service was always a striking lesson. Jesus knew that a great portion of life's disillusionment, despondency, and weariness came from a constant endeavor to minister to self. Naturally, men grow tired when wrapped in selfishness. The face of selfishness is not a rested face. It is surely not a happy one. Jesus pointed out the remedy. It is summed up in His words suggesting helpfulness. The best rest for the weary comes through ministering to others who are weary. "Men ask for a rainbow in the cloud; but I would ask more from Thee. I would be, in my cloud, myself a rainbow — a minister to others joy," said George Matheson. It is not easy, this business of ministering to others joy, but it is most satisfying and rewarding. Loneliness is overcome by befriending all. Sorrows become lighter when we attempt to lift the burdens of the afflicted. We have spent too much time considering the intake. We fail to see that what we yearn after comes by way of the output.

How many dark spots dot our pathway of service! There was the person whom we knew to be desperately sick. We were aware of the unfinished work in that home, the tired ones who ministered, the desire for companionship, and words of comfort, but we were too busy. We had many activities and numberless places to go. Time would not permit the visit we knew should have been made. Then when death intervened we remembered by way of flowers. An illustration of this neglect came from the lips of a splendid young man following the death of his father.

LIFE BEGINS WITH JESUS

It was so indelibly imprinted in my mind, that shortly after I wrote the poem, "Too Late."

> Tonight as I sit in my study,
> I ponder with sadness of heart
> The words from a life crushed by sorrow,
> That touched me and will not depart.
>
> It happened today, as I entered
> A home that death's hand had made bare,
> And stood in the midst of the mourners
> To offer a comforting prayer.
>
> The flowers were heaped on the casket,
> And after the prayer had been said,
> They gathered, surrounded by lilies,
> To look once again on their dead.
>
> 'Twas then came the words full of meaning,
> Words spoken in sorrow, not hate,
> "They did not come near through dad's illness,
> They sent him their flowers — too late!"
>
> "Too late!" What a sad, dreary message!
> How cruel its hollow refrain,
> To torture the hearts torn by sorrow,
> Increasing, not easing their pain!
>
> I thought of how heedless and selfish
> We are to our friends, small and great,
> To walk past their door when they need us,
> Then send them our flowers — too late!

As we look back, we also become conscious of the young person we knew to be in trouble. To that youth it was a matter of life and death. To us it was the result of sin. We carefully drew our robes around us and continued our self-complacent way. What an opportunity missed! What a chance to be of service! We might have helped to build a great future upon

PAUL'S CLEVEREST SAYING

that single mistake. That is what the Master did and what He requires of us.

His was the spirit of love. Service cannot be successfully rendered apart from this. He not only stressed its necessity but consistently practiced it. Love's test comes in our willingness to give, He said. "For God so loved the world, that He gave. Greater love hath no man than this, that a man lay down his life for his friends." He freely gave of Himself during His ministry. Never was His love withheld; never did it stop. Love led to Calvary, but He made no attempt to detour.

He, however, taught that love was more than a matter of giving. It meant forgiving as well. Without the latter it could not be complete. Men have always given their lives for their loved ones, friends, and nation. Love to be genuine must go deeper. "Love your enemies, bless them that curse you, do good to them that hate you, and pray for them which despitefully use you, and persecute you." This was love climbing the heights. It is what men were not willing to do, but what He gladly did. Bishop Whipple, known as the "Apostle to the Indians," once said, "For thirty years I have tried to see the face of Christ in those with whom I differed." This is the spirit of the Master, and on the cross He prayed for His persecutors, "Father, forgive them; for they know not what they do." If we have not this spirit, warns Paul, we are none of His. This is not easy, but life will never become Christ-like until the spirit that was His becomes ours. As Anna Shipton writes:

LIFE BEGINS WITH JESUS

Say not, 'Twas all in vain,
   The anguish and the darkness and the strife;
Love thrown upon the waters comes again
   In quenchless yearnings for a nobler life.

The spirit of Christ was one of sympathy. Love is impossible apart from sympathy. "He had compassion upon the multitudes," are words that can never be divorced from His life. But His compassion was not confined to sorrow. He wept with the sorrowful, but He also wept over the sinful. The doom that must inevitably descend upon the hard-hearted, the self-satisfied, the unrighteous, was ever upon His heart. The multitude to whom He ministered were the common run of people such as those who daily cross our path. Many of them were shepherdless souls with no one to guide them. They could expect little from the religious leaders who made it a practice to pass by on the other side when confronted with the problems that sorely perplexed and burdened. Thus they were wandering aimlessly, trying to bravely face the fate that befell them.

How sad the pictures are that come from Europe! Perhaps the most pathetic are the hoards of helpless women, children, the sick and aged, Jew and Gentile, who are seen fleeing, with what worldly goods they can carry, from the forces of death and destruction that draw ever closer. Pathetic, because their poor, haggard, distorted faces reveal a greater tragedy taking place within. The Master looked upon faces such as that in His day. He sees them again not only in Europe, but in America.

PAUL'S CLEVEREST SAYING

War is not the only force that creates havoc and destruction. I think the Master looked with pity upon the destroyers as well as the destroyed. The religious leaders, the warriors, men of position and wealth, all came under His scrutiny. He pitied those who could rejoice in the midst of tragedy, for He knew what the day of accounting would mean. Compassion was ever upon His heart; it must be upon ours.

In the third place, the spirit of Christ is seen in His attitude toward the world. He yearned for its redemption. In the prayer He taught His disciples is the petition, "Thy kingdom come. Thy will be done on earth, as it is in heaven." The Kingdom of God would mean a redeemed world. His ministry and teaching ever led toward that ideal. He gave His life for its salvation. His great commission was, "Go ye into all the world," and redemption was the purpose. There was no other reason for His followers to advance. A redeemed world includes redeemed individuals, redeemed society, in fact, a redemption of everything out of harmony with the will of God.

To accomplish this required infinite patience. How patient the Master was! With what patience He ministered to the multitude! The hope of the world rested in them. He couldn't hurry. He couldn't abuse them for their slowness of heart. It was not His fault if they failed to understand. He used simple language, teaching them in parables and using as illustrations that which they saw and experienced daily. Always He stressed the purpose for which He came and the work they were to do. But His patience with the

LIFE BEGINS WITH JESUS

multitude was no greater than that which He showed His own disciples. They were to be especially trained. He did not lose heart at their lack of faith and was ever thoughtful of their needs. The training was slow, and He was conscious that His ministry would be short. Yet He did not go so far ahead but what they could follow.

Coupled with patience was hopefulness. The thought of universal redemption seemed such a hopeless thing. It still does. But where we lose faith, the spirit of Jesus soared; where we feel all roads are closed, Jesus saw a greater highway that could be opened. Who else could have seen victory from a cross? Who else, but the Master, could have dreamed of the conversion of the widespread paganism that faced Him everywhere? We wilt to think of the vast, unclaimed multitudes of our day; yet where He had but a handful of followers we are reinforced in our world evangelism by millions. We lose hope in the midst of opportunity. He possessed it in the presence of almost certain defeat.

The spirit of Christ is our supreme need. It will enable us to live life triumphantly, and make us as earnest for the establishment of the Kingdom as it did the disciples. The sense of futility that marks much of our thinking will disappear. Our faith will be enlarged. We will look out upon life, in spite of the present confusion, and see victory for righteousness as He did. Such a vision is impossible apart from soul growth. A flickering faith beholds a flickering, defeated world. It is said of the Apostles that they

PAUL'S CLEVEREST SAYING

turned the world upside down. The spirit of Christ, producing an abounding faith was responsible. They took Him and His way of life seriously. He was their authority. They conquered because they allowed the Divine and human to fuse and advance together. Their orders had been given, and they went forth, certain they would not be left alone to accomplish a seemingly impossible task.

But the world is not the only direction in which defeat seems apparent. Ironically enough, we behold it in our own lives. We do not blame ourselves for this. Neither would we confess that it was because we lacked the spirit of Christ. For many, complete mastery appears impossible. The shout of triumph that leaps from the pages of the New Testament does not escape our lips.

How natural it was for Jesus to live in the presence of God! Deep spiritual messages did not bother Him. He rejoiced in the fellowship He had with His Father. With shining face He left His place of prayer. Victory within was present many years before He voiced the words of victory from the cross. It is this spirit that will enable us to live life triumphantly.

The spirit of Christ will make us happy, hopeful Christians. A magazine, issued during the terrific bombardment of England, carried the picture of men, women, and children, sitting on the ruins of what was once their home. The message underneath read, "They are singing, 'There will always be an England.'" If that was true, it certainly expressed hope in

LIFE BEGINS WITH JESUS

the midst of desolation. If we remove this picture from its setting and apply it to the Christian life, we would have vividly presented what the spirit of Christ does for us. It enables us to sing amidst the bombardments of life. "If God would make manifest the fact that 'He giveth songs in the night, He must first make it night," said William Taylor. Only the spirit of Christ will enable us to sing in the night. It gives us hope and inner peace in the presence of our greatest loss. But it does more; it sends us forth to minister to the hopeless, despondent, discouraged souls who suffer as we have.

Jesus was the world's greatest optimist. In the hour of deepest gloom He beheld an unfading light and triumphantly predicted victory. But we, poor souls, always seem defeated! This was not the spirit of the Master. We must believe as He did and with patience and hope, unceasingly work for the fulfillment of His heavenly vision.

WHAT SHOULD WE LEARN FROM JESUS?

"Learn of me." — MATTHEW 11:29

THE INVITATION of which our text is a part indicates the desire of Jesus to bestow upon the weary that which life continues to deny them. "Come unto me all ye that labor and are heavy laden and I will give you rest." It seems incongruous that one would not be willing to accept. Yet many hesitate because, they say, too much is required. The first requirement is that we take the Master's yoke upon us. We rebel at the idea of a yoke. It indicates work, service, hardship. To be yoked with Him presupposes that a life unlike that which the world developes must be a part of the plan. The second thing Jesus expects is that we learn of Him.

As a rule we are not particularly interested in study, especially the subjects taught by Jesus, yet we are all learners. We have to be for the world is overrun with teachers. We cannot pick up our newspapers, read our magazines, listen to our radio, or step from our homes without listening to what they have to teach. Their appeal is made to all classes and all ages. Their message is exceedingly challenging, high-powered, and aimed to produce results. That which degrades is clothed in evening gowns and dress suits.

Everything seems to shriek, "Learn of me," but the end of these appeals secretly guarded by their teachers is too often destruction. Opposed to this

LIFE BEGINS WITH JESUS

is the greatest Teacher of all who spoke the words of our text. His way is the way of life; His message the most challenging, and His pupils the most desired in life's crisis hours. Let us not deceive ourselves into thinking that the world's propagandists have everything their own way. As a teacher Jesus is still the most successful and His honor students run into millions. That which He taught will live long after the palsied gospels of the world pass into decay. It is essential that we learn of Him.

These are not the only instructors we have, and the classrooms founded by unscrupulous men are not the only ones we attend. Life is a school. It needs no truant officer. Everyone attends its various classes. Its methods of teaching vary. Often for years only the lecture course is given. This is easy, in fact, so easy that the percentage of pupils guided by its words of wisdom is small. Sometime, however, each pupil is forced to enter the laboratory of experience. This is not easy and reveals too many who fail because they are unprepared. The lecture course apparently falls on deaf ears, but the laboratory of experience is not only the most effective but the most essential. It is here the greatest schoolmasters are to be found.

What an amazing teacher failure is! We might not sense the value of its lessons at once, but as we regain our poise we catch a clearer vision of the heights. "A man who does not know how to learn from his mistakes," remarked Henry Ward Beecher, "turns the best schoolmaster out of his life." Yet this is a common occurrence. Mistakes and failures are

WHAT SHOULD WE LEARN FROM JESUS?

the most painful but surest trails to the mountaintop of success. Disappointment is another teacher. It reveals the source of genuine happiness and joy. Pain is an unusually gifted instructor. It broadens sympathy, understanding, mutual helpfulness, and patience. Sorrow is the teacher feared most, yet is nearest the heart of God. "Despise not thy school of sorrow, O my soul," urged George Matheson, "it will give thee a unique part in the universal song." And it will if we allow it to teach us the lessons intended.

These teachers are not selected by distorted minds. They are not in the employ of the cruel or unjust. There are some who think so, and fail to appreciate the message taught or the life they have attempted to mold. There is a reason for their being in our midst, for they give meaning to life that would not be discovered otherwise. Without them life would be incapable of challenging the best in man or of making the most of those to whom it has given birth. If they were removed, civilization would be retarded, God's program defeated, and Heaven a goal rarely attained.

Jesus had the pupils of life's school on His heart when He said, "Learn of me." He came not to supplant these teachers but to make their message clear. He never promised that following Him would protect men from the severe tests of life's laboratory. He taught His disciples the proper approach to these experiences and the secret of mastering each lesson. Only in this way could they leave life's classrooms victorious.

LIFE BEGINS WITH JESUS

Strangely enough there are many who hesitate to learn of Him. They would rather be crushed by the problems of the laboratory than to rise triumphantly above them, yet He holds the only possible solution. These were His schoolmasters, too, and He knew how severe they could be, yet how essential they were in the molding of life.

What are we to learn from Jesus? First, because life is not easy, we must learn the secret of rest. Our thought is to make life comfortable and pleasant. That is being done very successfully in the material realm by way of inventions, but inventions cannot provide ease from the burdens that press upon our shoulders or the problems that arise within. The Bible is the Christian guide book and it does not suggest easy times even for those who love God, and it presents life as it is. The same suffering that has come to all men must come to us. The same difficult situations must be faced. This should not cause us to grow bitter or rebel against God, for these are opportunities. They harden us. Without them we would grow soft and become unfit for the Kingdom. But Jesus offered something to offset these hardships. He offered rest. Not rest from that which we feel might crush us, but rest in the midst of it. "Do not pray for easy lives! Pray to be stronger men. Do not pray for tasks equal to your powers. Pray for powers equal to your tasks. Then the doing of your work shall be no miracle, but you shall be a miracle," said Phillips Brooks. And is not that the meaning of life? Doctor Edward Judson once said, "We no longer believe in

WHAT SHOULD WE LEARN FROM JESUS?

Christ because of His miracles, but we believe in miracles because we believe in Christ." He can make a miracle of your life and mine if we but let Him, and that is a revelation of His power all will believe.

He stands ready to bestow rest because He knows the pathway before us. God has a plan for each life. This doesn't mean that every adverse wind is a part of His divine plan. It does mean, however, that every bitter experience can enlarge that plan. "We need not give thanks for everything," suggested Paul, "but we can give thanks for the blessings derived from every experience." Growth, childlikeness, faith, confidence in God, are the results of many experiences for which we could not offer prayers of thanksgiving. God had a plan for Jesus' life. The Master might not have given thanks for a cross raised by cruel hands, but He was thankful for what that cross would accomplish. Crosses are in our pathway, too, but a cross is always an opportunity. "For our light affliction, which is but for a moment, worketh for us a far more exceeding and eternal weight of glory; while we look not at the things which are seen, but at the things which are not seen," said Paul. And the things which are not seen are real. We might not be able to see the value of affliction. Certainly we wonder what the breaking of our hearts can mean to others. When the children of Israel wandered in the wilderness, and the years of hardship dragged on, they began to wonder what good would result from it, and even yearned for bondage again. That was because they could not see the land of promise.

LIFE BEGINS WITH JESUS

Sometimes the path leads through the wastes of loneliness. The last verse of a well-known poem by Belle E. Smith presents in a real and touching way the desire of a lonely heart.

> Oh, friends, I pray tonight,
> Keep not your kisses for my dead, cold brow —
> The way is lonely; let me feel them now.
> Think gently of me; I am travel worn;
> My faltering feet are pierced with many a thorn.
> Forgive, oh hearts estranged, forgive, I plead!
> When dreamless rest is mine I shall not need
> > The tenderness for which I long tonight.

What loneliness is contained in the word "exile"! What good could come from that? The Psalms did, together with faith in God that could not be shaken. Who has not been comforted by the twenty-third Psalm, and has not some time or another with wet eyes repeated, "Yea, though I walk through the valley of the shadow of death, I will fear no evil for thou art with me"? No man could write words as significant and touching as these without first going through the valley of some tragic experience.

A prison is hardly the place toward which we look for revivals. Yet it was a common occurrence in the days of the early church. Someone was always being greeted on their return from imprisonment where they had spent the hours of their incarceration preaching Christ. The Apostle Paul, slowly dying in a dungeon, was not content to sit and wait for death. Feverishly he worked, writing letters to the churches until his hands became numb, and his eyes refused to remain

WHAT SHOULD WE LEARN FROM JESUS?

open. The best of the Negro spirituals were born in the dark, cruel days of slavery. Most of the hymns that deeply touch us came as a result of suffering.

A cross in the pathway of God-touched men is always a prelude to something greater. Without it resurrections are impossible. Jesus knows the pathway before us and bids us learn of Him that we might gain assurance of the value of that road.

He is aware of our unused powers. He knows the limits to which we can go. He is also conscious of the great possibilities of our life that have never been expressed. The greatest unused power is that which we have not released. God demands its use for it was never meant to be hoarded. It is earth that needs it, not Heaven. To fail the world in this respect is to fail Him. Have we not marveled at the faith Jesus had in His disciples? That faith was not the result of wistful thinking. He had reasons for it, and that is the same faith He has in us. "Faith is to believe what we do not see, and the reward of this faith is to see what we believe," said St. Augustine. And this is not theory, but fact. Blessed is the man who can see what he believes.

Jesus knows that we are equal to the greatest tragedies life can send upon us. They will not overwhelm us if our life is Christ-centered, for our unused powers were meant for that purpose. We will never know what is inside of us until we face the fiercest storms, then, for the first time, we will realize how others prevailed at the place we feared most. We thought it was impossible, but Jesus did not. He

LIFE BEGINS WITH JESUS

knew, and that is why He called men to seemingly impossible tasks. That gave the Christian church its birth. It will also give us a new birth.

There are secrets we will not learn until sorrows enter our lives. Jesus will never be as precious to us as He is then, and our loved ones will never seem nearer. Heaven will become as real as earth. It is true that this assurance does not come immediately. It takes time and patience to adjust ourselves to any situation, and sorrow is the most difficult. We can well understand why the author of the poem, "A Little Way," ends with these words:

> Although it seems so very, very far
> To that dear home where my beloved are,
>   I know, I know,
>   It is not so;
> Oh! give me faith to feel it when I say
> That they are gone — gone but a little way!

That is why rest is needed. It enables us to get our bearing. To accomplish this Jesus invites us to learn of Him.

In the second place, we should learn of Jesus the necessity of prayer. The reason for one of His parables was that "men ought always to pray, and not to faint." He recognized this as man's supreme need; his greatest source of strength. It was not repetition of words He stressed, for that He continually condemned. His prayer life reveals how much can be accomplished by short prayers if fellowship with God remains unbroken. The prayer He taught His disciples is exceedingly short, yet how comprehensive in scope!

WHAT SHOULD WE LEARN FROM JESUS?

This was the vital factor in His ministry. He prayed as though every moment of His life depended upon it — and it did. Sometimes it took the form of quiet meditation. On other occasions He prayed in agony. It depended upon the need.

The rapid development of early Christianity can be summed up in the words following Pentecost, "They preached the word with boldness." That boldness was not a coincidence. Many things combined to produce fearlessness on the part of the Apostles, but the revitalizing of their prayer life was a tremendous factor. Peter was one of the leaders, yet he was never considered bold, previous to this, in spite of the Master's faith in his ability. Now, however, he was the most courageous of all. That which is true of him is likewise true of those who worked with him, and the answer is to be found throughout the book of Acts. It was the result of prayer.

In the third place, we need to learn of Jesus the power of love. Why does God's plan of life lead through pain, sorrow, and loneliness? Why does Jesus expect so much of us, even insisting that a cross should not be evaded? The reply of the world would not be flattering, but to the Christian there can be only one answer — love. God chastens because He loves. "What mortal mind can realize the full significance of the position to which our God lovingly raises His little children? He seems to say, All my resources are at your command,' " said F. B. Meyer. They are, yet we snap at Him and sullenly ask, "What has He done for me?"

LIFE BEGINS WITH JESUS

Jesus demanded much of His disciples because of His great love. Love seeks to make life perfect, and a perfect life is impossible apart from the forces that cut deep. We might question much, but we cannot deny the love that is behind every experience. George Matheson didn't write, "O love that wilt not let me go" as a beautiful poem. He wrote it because in his sudden blindness he felt that love and it was that which gave power to his life and ministry.

But love brings its problems to the lover as well as the one loved. God suffers when we suffer. He feels the pain that is upon our heart. The Saviour who wept during His earthly ministry is just as tender-hearted today. The trying situations in which we are placed do not go unnoticed or unfelt. That is why the Bible contains so many precious promises. It is the Lover reaching out His strong arm to place around those He loves.

Perhaps we can understand the love of God better when we consider the heart-breaking experiences that come with our own love, for the greater our love the greater our pain. It is love that brings sorrow. We may pity another because of their loss, and do everything humanly possible to help them, but the sorrow that tears at our heart will come at the point of our greatest love. These words by Whittier have comforted me in that they sum up so perfectly the love and tender ministry of my wife:

> The blessings of her quiet life
>   Fall on us like the dew.
> And good thoughts where her footsteps pressed,
>   Like fairy blossoms grew.

WHAT SHOULD WE LEARN FROM JESUS?

> Sweet promptings unto kindest deeds
>   Were in her very look;
> We read her life as one who reads
>   A true and holy book.
> We miss her in her place of prayer,
>   And by the hearth-fire's light;
> We pause beside her door to hear
>   Once more her sweet "Good-night!"
> Fold her, O Father! in thine arms,
>   And let her henceforth be
> A messenger of love between
>   Our human hearts and thee.

Finally, we need to learn of Jesus the certainty of life everlasting; not simply that there is a life beyond. We must be as sure of it as He was. Nowhere do we find Him trying to justify His belief in Heaven. He offers no arguments; He raises no questions. He was so sure He talked as though it were a neighboring town with which He was always familiar, or a house that He knew from cellar to attic. This is the assurance we need today. That will give meaning to every experience. We might have untold troubles on the road, but the Home beyond, presented by Jesus, justifies every hardship encountered. Why should the road be smooth? We never fully appreciate that which has been placed in our hands without effort on our part. Heaven is so superior to anything else that we should rebel at nothing that will sharpen our appreciation when we approach it. The genuine shout of joy in that day will not come from the lips of one pampered by this world, but from the Christian, who, like the Master, has tasted the bitter as well as the sweet.

LIFE BEGINS WITH JESUS

Even in this life there are many things that become clear only as we look back. We do not understand them now. We do not know the reason, but when our mind has cleared and we look back it begins to dawn upon us. Not everything, perhaps, but enough to realize the good that came to us. But from Heaven every turn of life's road will be understood. We will wonder why we didn't see it before. It will be as plain as the land we now so dimly see. We might not appreciate the happenings of yesterday or understand their meaning, and it is for that reason we need to learn of Jesus. In the poem, "The Meaning of Yesterday," I have sought to present values so often overlooked.

> Yesterday came with its sunlight and shadows,
> Scattering happiness, fostering strife;
> Now with its passing we search for the answer,
> What did our yesterday mean to our life?
>
> Yesterday came with its doubts and its failures,
> Shaking foundations that long held secure;
> But in the hush of the night, faith had taught us,
> Only through Christ come the things that endure.
>
> Yesterday came with its sorrows to open
> Deeper and wider the wounds of our heart;
> Bitter our anguish, yet clear was its message,
> Life would be feeble had sorrow no part.
>
> Yesterday came with its clouds and its sunshine,
> Weaving together both laughter and tears;
> Yet in the twilight we read what was written,
> Yesterdays fit us to master the years.

Learning of Jesus does something to our life. It

WHAT SHOULD WE LEARN FROM JESUS?

makes us confident, optimistic Christians. It does something to our outlook on life. It enables us to see it from a new angle. We look through His eyes and go forth to love and serve as He did. "The true way of softening one's troubles is to solace those of others," said Madam de Maintenon. It is not always easy, but is a ministry that has no equal. It does something to the problems we face. We forget the fear and terror that once gripped our hearts, and view them now as great opportunities. It does something to our forward look. We know where we are going and are sure of what awaits us. "For here have we no continuing city," said the writer of Hebrews, "but we seek one to come." Indeed we do and this knowledge is made possible because of the One who invited us to learn of Him.

THE WORLD'S GREATEST NEED
"I am the way." — JOHN 14:6

WE WILL perhaps never realize how indebted we are to the misfortunes of others. The tragedy that has every appearance of striking the final blow has turned out, in the course of time, to be the instrument through which the world has been blessed. Every step upward in the progress of civilization has come as the result of suffering. "Christ's blessing ofttimes means sorrow, but even sorrow is not too great a price to pay for the privilege of touching other lives with benediction. The sweetest things in the world today have come to us through tears and pain," said J. R. Miller. They have, and it is this that makes them priceless.

This is even more pronounced in the realm of religion. That which strikes us most forcibly in the Old Testament, lifts us a little higher, or sends us forth with confidence in the goodness of God, was haltingly scribbled by some hand led on by a weary, troubled mind and broken heart. Tears do not dim the eyes of a devout life without creating a sensitiveness to God that never before existed.

That which is true of the Old Testament is likewise true of the New. Were it not for life's pain many things would never have been written. The fourteenth chapter of St. John has perhaps held more hope for the followers of the Master than any other. We do not know that Jesus would have started with these words, even on His last night, were it not for

LIFE BEGINS WITH JESUS

the anxiety easily detected upon the faces of His disciples. He was always conscious of man's inner thoughts. He had emphasized the fact that He was to leave them, and the effect of His words were evident. They were puzzled and alarmed. They showed it by their words as well as expressions. Every question that fills man's mind when separation comes was upon theirs. It was not a happy occasion. It was the hour of tragedy, and they were desperately attempting to reconcile themselves to the stunning news of His departure and vision the home He had just revealed and to which He was going.

We think of life everlasting on occasions, but when a loved one is taken from us we make a microscopic examination of Heaven. Ordinary glasses no longer satisfy, and as the examination continues we store up within our hearts, not notes from a classroom or text books, but confident assurance based upon experience. This reveals for the first time the little thought we have actually given immortality. Even though we have always been firm in our belief, have preached it and discussed it freely, we have done little more than scratch the surface. We have not sought out the details of that life as carefully as the life we now live. Our way has been happy and care free. This life has held us closely. Its problems have sometimes baffled us, to be sure, but we have never stopped learning or investigating, and in that we have but followed the thought of the world. A damper, however, has been placed upon too close thinking of the hereafter. Even religious circles have

THE WORLD'S GREATEST NEED

considered it unhealthy. In that they are wrong, all wrong. This life is not an end and to make it that is a serious mistake. We must know all there is to know about Heaven, or when death does come to our home we are unprepared. It is well for us to speak of the fascination of this life, but life everlasting should be more fascinating if it is to be richer than that which we now live, and we who are followers of Jesus know that it is. The practical course is to live as He did, extremely conscious and certain of both worlds at once.

It would not be unkind to say that the evident distress of the disciples and the Master's awareness of it was a blessing, for out of that experience came these words that have strengthened the living and comforted the dying. Their perplexity did not end with the revelation of His departure, and for that we also are thankful. Thomas said, "Lord, we know not whither thou goest; and how can we know the way?" Again, a problem that weighed upon them, a burden that pressed upon their hearts, brought from His lips the contents of our text, "I am the way."

That was an unusual claim, yet knowing Jesus as we do, we feel that it would be unusual if He had not said something electrifying. His words only take on added meaning when we look at His own insecure position. He, too, was following a way. A few more steps and the end would be reached. A short walk through Gethsemane, a short but painful journey up Calvary's hill, then a cross. This is an end of the way as the world viewed it. Yet knowing that, He

LIFE BEGINS WITH JESUS

disregarded it with a wave of His hand and with calm assurance asserted, "I am the way."

That was the spirit He possessed and portrayed throughout His ministry. Everything, even His own words, reveal how limited His path had been when judged by earthly standards. His disciples were untrained men. Some of them were unlikely prospects when first called. The money received was hardly sufficient to carry on His ministry. Luxuries were unknown. His success, when judged by converts was not great. Opposition mounted so rapidly that both influence and numbers seemed to be on the other side. Yet with assurance the disciples failed to share, He said that He was the way. What appeared to be the end of a hard, trying, bitterly opposed ministry, was completely overlooked by Him. That which seemed to be failure with the enemy in command was ignored. But as the Apostle Paul said, "The foolishness of God is wiser than men." We might not understand His ways, or appreciate the situation in which He allows us to remain, but He in His wisdom knows, and like Jesus we must trust and follow His leading. "Each of us may be sure that if God sends us on stony paths He will provide us with strong shoes," said MacLaren, "and He will not send us out on any journey for which He does not equip us well." God sent Jesus and adequately equipped Him for just such a task.

Have you ever been lost in a crowd? In a large city perhaps you have. Not that you forgot the way home, but you were lost because you knew no one

THE WORLD'S GREATEST NEED

and a sickening sense of loneliness came over you. Thousands of faces, but they all passed without glancing your way. This is a dreary experience, but it does not approach the experience that comes with being lost while in the presence of friends. You have perhaps had this happen, too. It was due to something that tugged at your heart. On numberless occasions you have been happy and content with the same group, but now, momentarily, your little world has tumbled around you. Disheartening news or a sudden tragedy has overtaken you, and you made an attempt to appear interested in everything taking place, but all the while you felt hopelessly lost. You were searching for a way, a way out of your difficulties. That was the experience of the disciples that night. They were lost. Simply to find any way was not enough. It was the right way they were searching after and suddenly it opened for them as it always does for us. It came when He said, "I am the way." It was in Him that hope was to be regained. In Him they were to go forth to minister. He was the way.

Jesus is both direction and road. He is direction in the sense that He points out where to go. His entire ministry centered around directing life to God, setting wayward feet upon the right highway, pointing out the only way of life, but that wasn't all. A sign post might show us where to go, yet be a very impartial thing. The person who directs us by pointing out the road is a time saver and often a life saver, but we still have to make the trip alone, and there is always a possibility of losing our way again.

LIFE BEGINS WITH JESUS

Jesus, however, was more than direction. He was the way itself, and running clear through the Gospels, after every direction, was the invitation to follow Him. It was not always given in these words, but the meaning was clear-cut and understandable. He was the direction, the road, and the companion on the journey, and it would be well to consider a few of the results of following Him.

In the first place, He is the way to an understanding of the will of God. We hear many people speak of the will of God and we usually receive the same impression. There is a lack of enthusiasm in their voice. They are not happy, and as we review our own lives we become conscious that we, too, have associated God's will with the unexpected and unwanted. It is something which we must meekly and helplessly accept.

To be sure, when Jesus uttered the words, "Not my will, but thine, be done," it was on just such an occasion. It was the hour when He knew the cross could not be side-stepped. We have listened to these words and remember them, but we have forgotten everything else.

Often that which we ascribe to the will of God is the result of our own sin. Not long ago I received a letter telling of the death of a young man who possessed great promise, but that was only one-third of the story. Not many years ago, three young men started drinking to excess. It soon led to the death of one, perhaps the weakest. His untimely passing made little impression upon the two remaining. Then

THE WORLD'S GREATEST NEED

came the letter describing the death of the second from the same cause. The third was later sent to a neighboring hospital and warned that He could not live if he continued. These boys were deeply religious, never missing the services of their church. And no doubt as they faced the future, repeating their prayers, they said, "Thy will be done." Yet, God was not responsible. It is not His will that promising young men should drink themselves to death. It is a cruel injustice to blame Him for the tragedies we bring upon ourselves.

The model prayer Jesus gave at the beginning of His ministry has within it the phrase, "Thy will be done in earth, as it is in heaven," and we repeat it every Sunday. Would that indicate His will was something over which to grit our teeth and attempt to bear?

From Him we learn that the will of God was meant for the making of a full, rounded, abundant life. Everything in the world we love has been willed by God. The blessing of rest; that which provides peace and happiness; the joyful hours and experiences are all the result of God's will. It is this that makes life so worth living that when the unaccustomed shadows fall, the difference seems more than we can bear. On this earth shadows must fall, sickness come, and reverses occur. We will have our share of sorrow. Jesus has taught us that God's will is in the former as well as the latter. And the pleasant, happy hours consume at least three-fourths of our life. How thoughtless we are, then, to overlook the vast amount

LIFE BEGINS WITH JESUS

of sunshine and infer that He wills only the darkness.

In the second place, Jesus is the way through our baffling problems. When darkness does descend, He becomes the light. Annie Johnson Flint says:

> I prayed for light; the sun went down in clouds,
> The moon was darkened by a misty doubt,
> The stars of heaven were dimmed by earthly fears,
> And all my little candle flames burned out;
> But while I sat in shadow, wrapped in night,
> The face of Christ made all the darkness bright.

It is this light that guides us through the maze of problems that confront us. Jesus is not only the light but He comes to our assistance. He helps us and as we lean on Him strength returns and darkness disappears.

Sin is one of the world's greatest problems. It touches all in one form or another. He is the way out of unrighteousness for He stands always ready to offer forgiveness and salvation.

Weakness is another baffling problem. A weak body with its physical handicap, a weak mind with its tragic results, weakness in the moral realm that makes one an easy prey to wrong, all are real — as real as life itself. But Jesus is the way. These are the very souls to whom He ministered and in each case He gave a renewal of hope. "God hath chosen the weak things of the world to confound the things which are mighty," said Paul. And C. H. Spurgeon testifies, "I bear my willing witness that I owe more to the fire, and the hammer, and the file, than to anything else in my Lord's workshop. I sometimes ques-

THE WORLD'S GREATEST NEED

tion whether I have ever learned anything except through the rod." Strength is the Master's answer to weakness and the source of that strength is in Him.

He is the way out of our tragic experiences. He gives assurance, one of the greatest assets when tragedy descends. He increases faith, the only foundation that will sustain. He bestows peace, to calm the troubled heart and ease the worried mind. He revives happiness even in the darkest hours.

In the third place, Jesus is the way to dauntless courage. These thoughts are being written while words concerning the failure of the church are still fresh in my memory. They were spoken only a short time ago by one who was so taken with the success of wordly enterprises that the church in his mind paled into insignificance. He had lost heart and judged the church and Christianity from his own distorted picture.

It is easy even for the faithful to lose courage. In the early days, Hermas lost courage when he viewed the church, and as a result saw her as a tottering old woman ready to fall. But as he looked closer, he noticed that she suddenly became beautiful and young, and he asked the reason, to which an angel replied that he saw the church at first from a heart grown worldly, that had lost its spirit of expectancy. But God had given him more faith and now he saw her as she really was. When courage is lost the church seems powerless, but this was not the spirit of Jesus. He was the way to courage, and turning to His wavering disciple He said, "Thou art Peter, and upon this rock I will build my church." Think of His courage!

LIFE BEGINS WITH JESUS

Daring to build His church on a foundation as insecure as that! And He still has the same courage, and continues to build His church on such raw material as you and I.

We lose courage in many other directions. We begin to sag as we consider this world, struggling under its heavy burden of war and continual destruction. Yet the Master had courage enough even in His day to predict its redemption.

Among the preachers of early Methodism, who faced persecution equal to that experienced by the first followers of Christ, was Thomas Lee. Upon his deathbed, he looked back over the years of his ministry; felt again beating upon his body the stones that had all but taken his life; saw upon the streets of many towns in which he preached the blood he had freely given. With this before his vision, he turned to his wife and said, "If at this moment I saw all the suffering I have had for His name's sake, I would say, 'Lord, if Thou wilt give me strength, I will begin again and Thou shalt add to them lion's dens, and fiery furnaces, and by Thy grace I will go through them all. " This is the courage engendered by the Master.

We lose courage as we face the forces arrayed against us, and weakly resign ourselves to them. I had the funeral sometime ago of the last Vineyard chanty-man of the old sailing ship days. Going to sea as a boy he sailed in whalers, eventually voyaging all over the world, attaining the exalted position of a chanty-man aboard a British trading ship. This

THE WORLD'S GREATEST NEED

office was the most desirable berth a sailor could obtain aboard old clippers and ships. The *Vineyard Gazette,* commenting upon his life, said, "As a chanty-man, he was depended upon to keep the courage of the toiling men from waning by singing lively songs. There was, in that day, a song for every principal activity aboard ship, from heaving in the anchor to mast-heading the light canvas, and the chanty-man had to know them all." He had to keep the courage of the toiling men from waning! How necessary this is today! Clipper ships and chanty-men have gone, but the need of courage is ever present. Jesus is still the way to courageous living. That office has never changed. "Be of good courage," He said to the fainthearted disciples, and later, in His last commission, "Lo, I am with you alway, even unto the end of the world."

Jesus is the way. We find this true throughout the Gospels. We experience it today. The early Christians were known as "followers of the way." He was alive. They were sure of that. He was in their midst. They were not following blindly, and the result was transformed lives. Those who witnessed this change in them and saw their courage knew that they had been with Him. "Followers of the way" became a part of common, every-day language. The most thrilling news is that He is just as much alive now as ever, and expects from us that which followed the transformation of His disciples. "Ah, yes," we admit, "but it is impossible to be always spiritually alert and active."

LIFE BEGINS WITH JESUS

Occasionally when we tap a man on the shoulder who looks downcast and ask, "What's wrong?" he answers, "Oh, I don't know, things are not as bright as they used to be. Maybe it's the weather." But it isn't the weather. We know that he has forgotten something. He has forgotten that Christ is still alive and is, as of old, the way for him. His shoulders have been burdened and he has suddenly found himself on a sidetrack, disillusioned and despondent.

Perhaps it is a woman. Her place is empty and we go to find out what is wrong. In spite of her assurance that nothing has happened, we can see by her face that she is not happy. She has failed to follow the way and things look different and she is not content.

If life is drab, and we are not the happy Christians we once were let us ask ourselves if we are a follower of the Way or have wandered off on a siding.

THE MASTER'S SPIRIT OF THANKSGIVING

"I thank thee, O Father, Lord of heaven and earth, because thou hast hid these things from the wise and prudent, and hast revealed them unto babes." — MATTHEW 11:25

JESUS WAS an example of continued sunny-heartedness. Let us forget the gloomy pictures of Him we have seen. They are the product of other years. Let us also forget, for today at least, some of the hymns still to be found in our hymn books. They were written when a Christian was judged largely by a long, sober face. Jesus tasted the bitter as well as the sweet. His pathway was one of sorrow, but He was never depressed. His heart was always overflowing with praise. His was a life of perpetual thanksgiving, yet He faced every tragic experience common to man. The most unusual thing about Him, and which is so often overlooked, is that in the midst of sorrow His spirit of thanksgiving reached new heights.

It is not hard to give thanks when the sun shines. People other than Christians are both happy and thankful under pleasant and smooth travel, but their spirit changes to one of gloom when storms overtake them. That is the child's attitude towards life. Children are always care free and happy when free from pain or unhampered by human restraint. But a child's smile can soon change to tears when faced with the unpleasant. They can be forgiven, for that is a part of childhood. Give them time, plus a few responsibilities and burdens, and a change slowly takes place.

LIFE BEGINS WITH JESUS

But when maturity is reached we look for something different.

There are, however, Christians who will not be in their places of worship today because the year has been unkind, and they are obsessed with the thought that there is nothing for which to give thanks. In fact, the happiness of others repel them. "If you carried the cross I carry," they say, "you would not be thankful either." Who hasn't heard this cry? We admit it is not easy. Crosses were never meant to be light, although some who become embittered have the easiest cross life can lay upon them. They have not caught the spirit of the Master. His life has not become a part of their life. He urged His followers to take a cross, not wait for one. He knew that genuine thanksgiving was impossible to him who had never experienced its weight.

During a conversation Froude remarked to Carlyle that God never seemed to show Himself in the affairs of men. Although Carlyle made many profound statements, on this occasion gloom overwhelmed him and he replied, "The worst of it is God never seems to do anything, Froude." It is this spirit that grips one the more he broods over his troubles. "The longer we dwell on our misfortunes," said Voltaire, "the greater is their power to harm us." "Yes," we add, "we know, for that experience has been ours." But it was never the spirit of the Master.

Jesus was not only the happiest but the most thankful person. His spirit of thanksgiving is found running throughout the Gospels. In the first place,

THE MASTER'S SPIRIT OF THANKSGIVING

He gave thanks for common things. In the story recording the feeding of the five thousand, we read that when Jesus took the loaves He gave thanks. Bread represents the common food of life. It was on the table of every home. Without doubt all had eaten it earlier that day. So had the Master and His disciples. Yet He looked upon it as the greatest gift God could bestow, and thanked Him as He held it in His hands. That loaf held by the Master reveals to us a great reason for our thankfulness. We are not always thankful for the common things and the ordinary experiences. Supposing, however, these everyday pleasures should suddenly be taken from us.

Have we thought of life apart from bread? If we haven't, let us remember that thousands of people will starve in Europe this winter because they will not have the bread that we carelessly toss away when the meal is over. Bread is life and the absence of it is death. Later in the spring we will see pictures of little babies and children like our own, naked and with bloated stomachs, thrown in piles waiting to be buried.

Bread is not the only gift which we fail to value and for which thanks are unsaid. Life is full of that which is common, yet fails to enthuse us. The Bible is life's most precious book. It always has been. What comfort would one with a broken heart receive were it not for the Bible? The promises contained in God's Word come as streams of living waters, flowing through what without it would be desolate wastes. "O Man," pleaded C. H. Spurgeon, "I beseech you

LIFE BEGINS WITH JESUS

do not treat God's promises as if they were curiosities for a museum, but use them as every-day sources of comfort." And that is what He intended them to be. God suffers, to be sure, when His promises go unread, but the ones who suffer most are ourselves. What is wrong with us that we allow our Bibles to rest upon our tables, unread, collecting dust? Shame on us, to treat God's Word with such callousness! It is common, yes, but its message is not. The Word is the bread of life to our souls, and we need it as often as we do bread for our bodies.

The church is the world's greatest institution. Have you thanked God for it today? If not, you should. You probably have, but what of the millions who pass its doors without even pausing to look. The influence of one man in neglecting the church caused a nation to sin and continued disastrously for generations. He was one of the few who could remain at home and still live righteously. But thousands, following His example, deteriorated spiritually the moment they left God's House. They were weak, and when the restraining hand of the church was removed, their downfall became complete. This was grievous unto Jotham, but that which wounded his heart most came within his own home. His son, Ahaz, following his father's example, not only became morally bad, but involved his nation in ruin. All this because one man thought it unnecessary or unimportant to attend church.

The church is not common to those whose physical handicaps prevent them from going. If we could

THE MASTER'S SPIRIT OF THANKSGIVING

take the scoffers to the homes of shut-ins and invalids that they might peer through the windows, glimpsing the expressions on the faces of all who today cannot attend divine worship, perhaps they would see the church in a new light.

Even our homes and loved ones are sometimes accepted as though they would always exist, yet God only knows the day when they will be removed and with them will go everything we cherish. If you have not thanked God recently for the person by your side do it today.

> What silences we keep, year after year,
> With those who are most near to us and dear!
> We live beside each other day by day
> And speak of myriad things, but seldom say
> The full, sweet word that lies just in our reach
> Beneath the commonplace of common speech.
> Then out of sight and out of reach they go —
> Those close, familiar friends who loved us so;
> And sitting in the shadow they have left,
> Alone with loneliness and sore bereft,
> We think with vain regret of some fond word
> That once we might have said and they have heard.

But we did not do it then, and now we must continue ever thinking of what might have been.

Jesus is common, too, in the eyes of a vast multitude. Even some who listened to His words were unimpressed. Many in the multitude whom He fed with the loaves and fishes never followed Him. When dying upon the cross He was jeered and ridiculed. "The greatest affliction that can befall a man is the unkindness of a friend," said Henry Fielding. Al-

LIFE BEGINS WITH JESUS

though I cannot follow him at this point, I know it must have been a heart-breaking experience for the Master to have watched those who had expressed friendship for Him depart from His presence in the hour of His greatest need, or take their places with the multitude crying, "Crucify!" Yet He is the One who has bestowed upon life all that is worth while. He treated everything, however common, as though equal to the greatest gift God could bestow.

In the second place, Jesus gave thanks in the face of apparent defeat. This is the hour one is apt to forget. He becomes overwhelmed by his lack of success. But this did not destroy the Master's spirit of thanksgiving. Our text is taken from an incident following the imprisonment of John the Baptist. He had just sent his disciples to Jesus with his last message in the form of a question, "Art thou he that should come, or do we look for another?" After reassuring the messengers and sending them back to John, Jesus revealed the pain that had been in His heart for some time. He knew what faced this bold prophet, yet nothing could be done to secure his release. God's program had received a serious blow. It was an hour of defeat for righteousness. It always is when a good man is removed. It was a time of personal anguish, but it didn't end there. Jesus realized that the towns in which He had wrought His greatest miracles and done His best work had not repented. He had been unsuccessful. It was in the midst of this seeming defeat that He lifted His voice in a prayer of thanksgiving. He did not thank God

THE MASTER'S SPIRIT OF THANKSGIVING

for what had happened to John or for the poor results of His mission. This is what He said, "I thank thee, O Father, Lord of heaven and earth, that thou didst hide these things from the wise and understanding and didst reveal them unto babes."

This is a strange Thanksgiving prayer to be sure, but so much like the Master. Herod was considered wise by those over whom he ruled. He had cast a prophet of God in prison, later to have him beheaded because he dared to reveal a hideous sin in high places. With all his supposed wisdom, he did not understand that John held the key to a better world than he had ever dreamed of, much less sought to create. To him this prophet was a meddler who pointed an accusing finger in his direction. The leaders of the sinful cities refusing to repent were looked upon as wise and prudent. They had reached maturity, but their knowledge was their undoing. Pride filled their hearts. It barred them from the kingdom. But while this was going on Jesus knew that those who did not possess worldly wisdom were trying to learn of Him. The wise went their self-satisfied way. It was the way of destruction. The untrained and unlettered sought the way that led to life. These thoughts must have been His on another occasion when He said, "Suffer the little children to come unto me, and forbid them not: for of such is the kingdom of God."

Jesus found something for which to be thankful in the face of seeming defeat. "The great thing is to suffer without being discouraged," said Fenelon. It

LIFE BEGINS WITH JESUS

is, though admittedly hard. If we have faced defeat this year, we need not give thanks for it, but that should not cause our expression of thanksgiving to cease. We still possess much. Hopeful signs abound everywhere. Like the Master, let us give thanks for them. That is the kind of thanksgiving God is waiting to hear. A verse by Johann A. Rothe expresses this thought:

> Though waves and storms go o'er my head,
>   Though strength and health and friends be gone,
> Though joys be withered all, and dead,
>   Though every comfort be withdrawn,
> On this my steadfast soul relies, —
>   Father! Thy mercy never dies.

In the third place, Jesus gave thanks in the presence of life's deepest pain. The reference for this prayer is found in John's Gospel. Lazarus was dead. Martha and Mary, the broken-hearted sisters, sent for Jesus. They knew He held the answer to this which mystified and overwhelmed them. The first thing He did in the presence of death was to give thanks. Lifting His eyes He said, "Father, I thank thee that thou hast heard me." He was thanking God for something that had not come to pass. "An active faith can give thanks for a promise though it be not as yet performed," said Matthew Henry, "knowing that God's bonds are as good as ready money." Jesus was sure of that, and His faith was so great that the thought of questioning whether or not God would answer never dawned on Him.

Have we ever trusted God so completely as to

THE MASTER'S SPIRIT OF THANKSGIVING

thank Him for that which we have not yet received? This is a vital part of thanksgiving, and calls for great faith. We thank Him for food before we eat it and we should, yet that doesn't require unusual faith. The food is before us. But have we dared thank Him in the morning for the strength we will receive during the day? Few ministers ascend their pulpits without praying for strength. But they go beyond this and thank God before the sermon is preached for the comfort that service will give to the weary and heavey laden; the spiritual victory that will come to someone tired of their sin. We do not think we are overoptimistic. That is the uppermost thought long before, when the sermon first begins to take shape. That is why the minister in touch with the Master always has a message. And Jesus gave thanks before He performed the miracle. But He did more than that. He caused a sorrowful home to burst forth in songs of thanksgiving. "Yes," we insist, "but it had every reason to. Lazarus returned again to life." That we know cannot happen in the same manner to our loved ones because Jesus has ascended unto the Father. But have we forgotten that He gave a hope to us as precious as that which He gave to Martha and Mary? This was the occasion on which He said, "I am the resurrection, and the life: he that believeth on me, though he die, yet shall he live; and whosoever liveth and believeth on me shall never die." Our Thanksgiving can be as joyous as Martha's and Mary's because Jesus promised even a greater life than that which He was now bestowing upon their brother.

LIFE BEGINS WITH JESUS

The best Lazarus could do was to remain with his sisters a few years more. I will admit these are precious years. We would give our possessions if by so doing our loved ones could remain a while longer. But even that pales into insignificance when compared with the assurance Jesus gave that we never lose our own. They are ours forever.

In the fourth place, Jesus gave thanks as He prepared for His own death. Each incident considered indicates ascending steps in His prayers of thanksgiving. This, I suppose, is reaching the heights. In the upper room, during the last supper, He took bread and blessed it and took the cup and gave thanks. To give thanks in view of the cross that will rise tomorrow is hardly to be expected. We would expect Him to give final instructions to His disciples. We are not surprised at His fervent prayer before the departure for the garden. Even the blessed promises of that night do not cause us to marvel. But to give thanks — that is different. Yet is it? Does not the spirit of thanksgiving fit into the pattern of His life as completely as instruction, prayer, and promises? And because Jesus gave thanks Christians have been doing it ever since. "God, forgive me," cried Charles Kingsley before his death, "but I look forward to it with an intense and reverent curiosity." And Paul, baring his soul, says, "I am in a strait betwixt two, having a desire to depart, and be with Christ." The last night holds no terror for the person who has walked through life hand in hand with the Master.

The thanksgiving spirit of Jesus continued after

THE MASTER'S SPIRIT OF THANKSGIVING

the supper ended. As they left for Gethsemane, He led the disciples in the singing of a hymn. And that hymn is significant. It was one of the Psalms and the Psalms grew out of a similar experience that now faced Him. As we read the Psalms we are immediately struck by the note of thanksgiving that runs clear through. Almost without exception they are hymns of praise, yet were written in the loneliness of exile. They spring from the hearts of men facing death in a foreign land. Strange, isn't it, that our greatest expressions of thanks have come from the tragic experiences of life that caused the children of the world to bitterly wail and complain? The disciples had not caught the complete meaning of thanksgiving when they entered the garden. That came later. It was not the seclusion of the upper room with Christ by their side, but persecution and death that caused them and the Apostles to sing anthems of praise. The same is true of the Christian church. Tribulation caused it to break into song.

I think you will find that the most thankful people are those who have passed through the deepest waters. The reason is clear. Every hour of pain and suffering makes the Christian conscious of the goodness of God. Our failures and defeats but underline the avenues of success proclaimed by the Master. Every friend and loved one momentarily lost brings Heaven nearer to our hearts. This is the source of genuine thanksgiving. Anything else is based on a foundation that must eventually be destroyed. It is only natural to give thanks for the material blessings that are ours, but if we do not climb higher heights than that, we haven't moved far from the path beaten by the world.

In the midst of our happiness today may we pause, not only to thank God for His blessings, but to remember others. Our Thanksgiving will be more Christlike if we think first of the suffering multitudes of the world: those broken in body and soul by war with its destructiveness; all who are on beds of pain, and those who are courageously attempting to bear a cross of sorrow. Secondly, we must remember Christ who made this day possible. Whatever blessings are ours this moment we owe to Him.

THE PEACE CHRIST GIVES
"Peace I leave with you, my peace I give unto you."
— JOHN 14:27

IF WE were to make our will and an unusual power given, guaranteeing that the one supreme thing we desired to give would be granted, what would that one gift be? Would it be wealth, freedom from pain and worry, or a life of continued happiness to our loved ones and the world? Some years ago my answer would have been different, perhaps, than now. Many things seemed of great importance then. But if that power were given me this moment, my answer would be — peace. I am sure no greater gift could be offered the world than that. Peace is the desperate need of every nation. Even when viewed apart from war, peace in the midst of turmoil and confusion that ever confronts life would be a blessing.

This is what I would likewise bestow upon my loved ones. Life is full of lonely, sorrowful, distressing experiences and our own must have their share. The one essential need in that hour is peace. If we possess peace we can conquer. An inner peace gives poise, calm, and assurance, no matter how bleak the future.

Jesus revealed the same need and His desire to provide a remedy in the closing moments of His ministry. He knew what was before Him, yet ignored that. He was concerned about the future of His disciples as He saw the dark, dreary, dismal, painful days that awaited them. He had the power not only to will what He would, but to guarantee its fulfillment. Thus He made His one bequest, that of peace.

LIFE BEGINS WITH JESUS

"Peace I leave with you, my peace I give unto you; not as the world giveth give I unto you. Let not your heart be troubled, neither let it be afraid."

During His ministry Jesus used the word "peace" in many ways. In the Sermon on the Mount He taught, "Blessed are the peacemakers: for they shall be called the children of God." On another occasion He urged His followers to be at peace one with another. To the angry waves He quietly said, "Peace, be still." To the sinful, "Go in peace." But these references do not suggest the type of peace that was upon His mind in the upper room. He was talking now about His peace, and the amazing thing is that He said more about His peace in the closing chapter of His life than He did at any other time. Yet those were the hours when storm clouds appeared everywhere. Judas had gone out into the night to betray Him. His leading disciple was boastful and self-confident. The rest were slow to understand. "Don't talk in proverbs to us," they insisted. He knew that before long they would all forsake Him and flee. The band of soldiers was organizing for His arrest. The cross was but a few hours away. Yet this was the time He talked most about His peace.

His enemies were planning to destroy whatever peace He had left. If any, they reasoned, it was little. But Jesus was talking to His disciples in terms of abundance. Perhaps it was well they didn't fully understand what His gift of peace would mean. They accepted it as they had everything He offered. They went from the upper room singing a hymn. But from

THE PEACE CHRIST GIVES

that night, peace as the world knew it was not theirs. Never again did they enjoy a ministry of walking beside quiet waters or rejoicing in the seclusion of an upper room. For the peace Jesus gave was the peace He possessed. It was not meant as an armistice to unrighteousness. The storms that surrounded the Master would surround them. They were not to escape. His gift was that of a sustaining peace within, while the raging forces of the world beat upon them unmercifully from without. Harriet Beecher Stowe says:

> When winds are raging o'er the upper ocean,
>   And billows wild contend with angry roar,
> 'Tis said, far down beneath the wild commotion,
>   That peaceful stillness reigneth evermore.

Common knowledge teaches us that one cannot give what He doesn't possess. The life of Christ demonstrated, however, that He had everything He promised. He never boasted or raised false hopes. When He said that in His Father's house were many mansions and He was going to prepare a place for us, we can accept it. When He spoke of Himself as the resurrection and life, we can be sure He meant it. If we are not sure of His promises, it is because we are not sure of Him. "Those who are readiest to trust God without other evidence than His word, always receive the greatest number of visible evidences of His love," said C. G. Trumbull. That is what the person with little faith misses, and is the reason for distrust and unnecessary questioning of His ability and effectiveness. The disciples might not have understood, but they had complete trust and confidence in Him. Therefore, when He promised peace, they did not raise questions, for they knew He possessed it. They knew, because almost daily during His ministry they had marveled at the inner peace He displayed. The times that called forth a flare of anger on the part of His followers, Jesus remained peaceful. When many upon whom He had showered His love grew cold and left, the disciples became greatly disturbed, but Jesus continued unperturbed. To the angry waves He spoke peace and they subsided. To the distressed minds, withered souls, and diseased bodies He uttered the same word and peace was always restored. There was no need for the disciples to question His gift of peace. They already knew. It is by way of experience that we corroborate His promises, and they possessed that experience. The New Testament reiterates repeatedly that we, too, can be in possession of that peace if we meet the requirements demanded. As we rush to qualify we make amazing discoveries.

In the first place, we become conscious of the kind of peace He offered. He said, "My peace I give unto you." What was His peace? Was it not the peace of obedient sonship? Peace does not come through disobedience. Scripture, which is a revelation of God's love, is also a commentary on the results of disobedience. The list begins with Adam and Eve, continues to the end, and reveals the same results — the absence of peace. Jesus came to do the will of His Father and was always obedient to that will. Even a cross did not cause Him to disobey.

How often we find the absence of peace in those

THE PEACE CHRIST GIVES

we know. When we examine their lives closely we discover that they are not obedient to God. In fact, is not that the same discovery we make when peace is lacking in our lives? We are reaping the fruits of disobedience. The lack of peace in the world is the result of a corresponding lack of obedience. Wars do not happen. They come because God's laws are discarded. Even when war does not exist we invariably find a restless multitude, running from one place of pleasure to another, indulging in one sin today, a different one tomorrow. Peace is found only as men turn to God and seek to obey His will.

The peace of Christ was also due to His unfailing confidence in His Father. Jesus never doubted, yet He had many reasons to. Even now, while seated with His disciples in the upper room, knowing the forces arrayed against Him, He could have wondered whether or not God cared, yet the words that were spoken by Him that evening revealed an unshaken faith and trust. A short time later, when He entered the Garden of Gethsemane and prayed in agony, becoming ever conscious that the cup placed before Him would not be removed, He did not doubt.

More and more have I come to learn that God knows what He is about. There is a bit of conversation from one of George MacDonald's books bearing upon this thought. "I wonder why God made me," said Mrs. Faber, bitterly. "I am sure I do not know what was the use of making me!"

"Perhaps not much yet," said Dorothy, "but then

LIFE BEGINS WITH JESUS

He hasn't done with you yet. He is making you now and you are quarreling with the process."

And isn't that human nature? It takes confidence in God — the brave assurance Jesus had — to remove our querulous, distrustful, attitude toward Him. We might not be able to explain everything that takes place, even in our own lives, but we know He always holds the answer. We do not doubt Him because of these experiences. As in the case of Jesus, we do not desert. Instead, we draw the closer, even though aware that a cross might loom in our pathway at any time. Ella Wheeler Wilcox has expressed this faith in the following verse from one of her poems:

> I will not doubt, though all my ships at sea
>   Come drifting home with broken masts and sails;
>   I will believe the hand which never fails
> From seeming evil worketh good for me.
>   And though I weep because those sails are tattered,
>   Still will I cry, while my best hopes are shattered:
>   "I trust in Thee!"

I once felt that Job was careless, that He hadn't thought as carefully as the case demanded when he said, "Though he slay me, yet will I trust in him," but that was when life led only beside the still waters. Triumphant faith in God is born of bitter experiences. Job wouldn't have given expression to these words if his heart had never felt the thrusts of sorrow. If Jesus had lived a sheltered, pampered life, He would not have been the Saviour. Whenever we desire to find an unshaken faith let us not search in the highways of ease. Instead, let us go to some upper room surrounded by

THE PEACE CHRIST GIVES

shadows or a Gethsemane bathed in tears. It is there we will find complete trust and confidence. It is there we will also find peace. "They tell me that I shall stand upon the peaks of Olivet, the heights of resurrection glory," said George Matheson. "But I want more, O my Father; I want Calvary to lead up to it. I want to know that the shadows of this world are the shades of an avenue — the avenue to the house of my Father." If we allow a Gethsemane and Calvary to lead up to the resurrection morn, we will not only enter the Father's house, but will be dispensers of faith, courage, and peace along the way.

The most amazing thing is that the peace of Christ remained in spite of His unlimited vision. Most of us cannot see beyond today. God has blessed us in that, and peace is based on the pleasant hours we now experience. But Jesus knew what was in tomorrow. Months before He had revealed the cross to His disciples. His was not the peace of blissful ignorance. It was a peace that came in spite of His knowledge.

We can be calm today because we have no reason for fear. But if suddenly our vision should enlarge and we saw suffering, sorrow, and even death before us, how peaceful would we be then? Jesus knew, yet His peace remained undisturbed. How rare and greatly to be desired is that peace! Would we not like to possess it? That is what He offers. It was "My peace" He talked of, not some other person's or the world's, and He offered it as a gift. No one need be denied. Although freely given it has not been widely accepted, perhaps for the reason that His

LIFE BEGINS WITH JESUS

gift of peace is impossible apart from Himself. We cannot have anything Christ possessed without having Him, and there are many who do not want Him.

In the second place, Jesus expected competition. He knew that those who followed Him would not have everything their way in keeping this peace. He realized how fascinating the world's peace was. His peace and the world's would be in constant conflict. He also knew that the followers of the world were more aggressive than were the righteous, and once said, "The children of this world are in their generation wiser than the children of light." He knew it counted no cost too great if at the end it could wean a child of God away from the light he possessed. And in the matter of peace it would not sit idly by. The world would immediately set before these disciples a more attractive, tempting, and savory dish. Jesus had gone through all that and He knew. On the eve of His ministry Satan offered Him peace as the world gave it. Three times He held before Him that which humanity always craved. They were tempting, flattering offers. They would be attained immediately. "Turn stones to bread." Think of the peace and contentment that would be His as a miracle worker! "Cast thyself down from the pinnacle of the temple.

Behold the kingdoms of the world." Yes, the world offers much to woo one away from God, and everything is placed upon the most tempting platter, while momentarily peace reigns over all. Pleasure, excitement, wild adventure, intemperance, indifference, moral looseness — how it clothes these in the gar-

THE PEACE CHRIST GIVES

ments of peace! But the world that gives so generously exacts a tremendous price. "You can have these things," said Satan to Jesus, "if you bow down and worship me." That is the price the world demands for its peace — the worship of evil, a devotee of that which leads only to destruction and ruin. It only tantalizes us with its gifts. It offers only because of the greater harvest in souls it will receive. Jesus recognized all that, and said to His disciples, "Not as the world giveth, give I unto you." Of course not. He came to overcome the world. His gift of peace was not temporary. It was not meant to tease that it might eventually destroy, but was a gift designed to lift and save. The more it was used the richer it became. It was the peace of God.

It was this the world had always tried to take from Him, but was powerless. Now, with only a few hours remaining, He could speak of "My peace." He still possessed it. A few hours more and a world that had no room for Him would nail Him to a cross, but it could not tear from Him His peace.

It has not ceased in this direction. A cartoon from the *Christian Advocate* of some months ago illustrates this. Christ is shown walking down a highway lined with Nazi soldiers. He is dressed in tattered garments, a crown of thorns upon His head, staff in hand. Passing Him, in a high-powered motor car, are two grinning, sneering men — Hitler and Goering. Underneath the picture were these words from the lips of Hitler, "There is no room for that chap in my new world, Herman!" The world not only is bent on

LIFE BEGINS WITH JESUS

banishing the Master, but on destroying His peace as well. But it cannot be done. Christ cannot be banished nor is peace taken from the hearts of His disciples.

Finally, He suggested that when His peace is accepted we can go through life free from fear and with an untroubled heart. "Peace I leave with you, my peace I give unto you; not as the world giveth, give I unto you. Let not your heart be troubled, neither let it be afraid." This sounds impossible. We think of the fear that must be upon the minds of His disciples in Europe at this hour. We cannot visualize a world such as this without seeing with it millions of troubled hearts.

Why did Jesus tell these disciples, whom He knew faced untold agony, not to be afraid or allow their hearts to become troubled? Because that is the thing for which His peace is designed. It is not a peace of inactivity, continued quietness, or passive resistance. That is what the world claims to offer. His was a peace for the storms of life. The experience that calls for fear is the hour for which this peace is intended. "Oh, happy are we if the hurricanes that ripple life's unquiet sea have the effect of making Jesus more precious," said MacDuff. "Better the storm with Christ than smooth waters without Him."

The island of Martha's Vineyard may be lashed by storms so severe that ships will not dare to leave their sheltered haven. But we do not fear, because we enjoy the peace that comes with the warmth and safety of our own homes. Yet we are actually in the

THE PEACE CHRIST GIVES

midst of the storm, surrounded as we are by water. May we picture His peace in much the same light. When the storms of life surround us a haven of safety is provided that banishes fear. We are in the midst of the storm, completely encircled, yet are at peace. As Annie Johnson Flint says in one of her poems:

I prayed for peace, and dreamed of restless ease,
  A slumber drugged from pain, a hushed repose;
Above my head the skies were black with storm,
  And fiercer grew the onslaught of my foes;
But while the battle raged, and wild winds blew,
I heard His voice and perfect peace I knew.

The peace of Christ was intended for the failures and defeats of life. If ever we become despondent and our stout heart begins to fail it is when we suddenly come face to face with defeat. "Do not get discouraged; it may be the last key in the bunch that opens the door," said Stansifer. Or as Maltbie D. Babcock said, "Trouble may demolish a man's business but build up his character. The blow at the outward man may be the greatest blessing to the inner man. If God, then, puts or permits anything hard in our lives, be sure that the real peril, the real trouble, is what we shall lose if we flinch or rebel." Yet we are so slow and dull in learning this lesson. Many never master it. I knew of a man who loved to walk beside the Charles River just outside of Boston. He would sit on its banks for hours watching the Harvard boatsmen as they went through their strenuous training. One day, almost without warning, his small fortune was wiped away. For some time he wandered through the streets dazed. Then one day he was

LIFE BEGINS WITH JESUS

missing, and shortly after they found his body floating in the river he loved. He was so possessed with stocks and bonds he had no time or room for the peace of Christ. Even sitting upon the banks of the peaceful Charles did not suggest to him he lacked within the one thing he loved most in his leisure hours — peace.

The peace of Christ is also intended for life's shadow hours. Even the thought of life's shadow hours chill us. Yet it shouldn't for His bequest in the upper room was intended for just such a time. It is only to be expected that visibility will be poor when shadows deepen. Our eyes do not readily accustom themselves to the dark. That is our trouble, we depend upon physical eyesight. We place our value upon what is seen. The Prophet Isaiah, speaking of the coming Messiah, said, "He shall not judge after the sight of his eyes," and as we follow the Master's life we realize how true this is. That is why He saw in people and in the world what others could not. As we enter the shadows, we, too, are not to judge after the sight of our eyes.

The Psalmist had his soul riveted upon God when he said, "Though I walk through the valley of the shadow of death, I will fear no evil: for thou art with me." Shadows cannot bruise us, not even the shadow of death. Yet because of our lack of faith and understanding, fear grips our heart and we are bruised and broken before death takes place. We are so dazed by death's shadow that we fail to see the Companion who is journeying by our side. Human experience has proved that a lingering shadow is

THE PEACE CHRIST GIVES

harder to bear than the results of the painful experience it indicates. The hours of waiting are intolerable. Nervous tension is great.

Our daylight experiences with Jesus should prepare us for the dark. What He always has been, He always will be. He bestows the same calm; He commands the same confidence; He gives the same peace. His companionship knows neither darkness nor light. Night raises no barriers to His presence. George Matheson in one of his prayers said, "Whether Thou comest in sunshine or rain I would take Thee into my heart joyfully. Thou art Thyself compensation for the rain."

Jesus reminded His disciples that He was the light of the world, and light is meant for darkness. If we can place a light in the midst of life's shadows, what else have we to fear? Surely not blackouts! They come only when we lose faith. It is then we seal the windows, hiding from us every ray of light the Master promised would be sent. We might not understand everything and the light might appear extremely dim to our weary, bloodshot eyes, but we will know and the waiting period is shorter than it seems. "God's afters' are worth waiting for," said G. Campbell Morgan. "However dark the 'now' is, there will be light in God's 'after' to explain the darkness."

Let us rest assured that it is in the shadowy valley that Christ looms the largest. It is there His peace becomes the more pronounced. In the hours feared most we hear Him say, "My peace I give unto you Let not your heart be troubled, neither let it be afraid."

OUT-LIVED SORROW
"Ye shall be sorrowful, but your sorrow shall be turned into joy." — JOHN 16:20

A FRIEND told me recently that when her mother died, she said to the family doctor, "I wish I could go to sleep and not wake up for a year." His answer was, "It would do you no good, for when you did awake you would still have to go through what you face now."

When our loved ones leave us, this desire, or some other akin to it, is universal. It is one of the first thoughts to take its place among the many that crowd in upon our bewildered mind, and is consequently the beginning of much we systematically reject. We who have passed through this bitter experience know that we must out-live sorrow. We cannot out-sleep it.

It often takes the unexpected and unwanted to provide a deeper appreciation of God and an attempt to understand what before appeared too remote. Death always brings us to our senses. Men who have ignored the messages of the prophets and treated lightly the teachings of Jesus, are suddenly aroused when death comes. That is a messenger known to be real and a message quickly understood. But when little thought has preceded its coming they are not ready. Is there any wonder they seek to out-sleep sorrow? But even when our life has been lived in the presence of God we are never fully prepared. Death is not a pleasant subject, and our own are so precious that the slightest thought of their passing leaves us as weak and frightened as the climax of a horrible dream.

Jesus said, "Ye shall be sorrowful, but your sorrow shall be turned into joy." He didn't mean that in some distant future, after the pain has left our hearts, our sorrow shall be followed by joy. That is what our well-intentioned friends tell us. This promise of the Master, however, is for now, the moment our sorrow is the keenest. It is natural that like Nicodemus we ask the question, "How?" And when we search for the answer we are amazed at what we discover.

In the first place, there dawns the realization that God never takes from us what He has given in love. Our loved ones are still ours. Death cannot remove them. It but keeps them, holds them for us, by carrying them into His presence. That which is precious can be lost in this life, but nothing precious can be lost in Heaven. "I have held many things in my hands," said Martin Luther, "and I have lost them all; but whatever I have placed in God's hands that I still possess." But Jesus goes beyond that when He says, "I give unto them eternal life; and they shall never perish, neither shall any man pluck them out of my hand." They are ours, and He who gave them to us intended that gift to be forever. Susan Coolidge presented the same thought in her poem, "Our Own."

> Our own are our own forever; God taketh not back His gift;
> > They may pass beyond our vision, but our souls shall find them out
> When the waiting is all accomplished, and the deathly shadows lift,
> > And glory is given for grieving, and the surety of God for doubt.

OUT-LIVED SORROW

> So sorrowing hearts, who humbly in darkness and all alone
> Sit missing a dear lost presence and the joy of a vanished day,
> Be comforted with this message, that our own are forever our own,
> And God, who gave the gracious gift, He takes it never away.

Sin can seriously damage, but not death. And the dear, righteous souls who have brought the presence of the Master deeper into our homes, have no fear of the penalties wrought by sin, and we easily brush that thought aside. This, however, we should not forget, that even though a gift of God, He did not promise that they would always remain with us here. That is what we expect, but God plans well and wise. He has a mission for every life. It is a high calling, and sometimes cannot be fulfilled in a few years. Let us rest assured that when God calls faithful servants He has a greater mission for them.

To be sure, we always feel that their most important work is here. When a young, active wife or husband is taken, leaving little ones, and a vacant place in the work of His church, we are apt to question His wisdom. Does not the home still need their unselfish devotion and tender care? What shall we say concerning the children, who demand and should have the loving ministry of understanding parents? Of course they are needed, but God can make other adjustments. He is doing that constantly. But that higher mission! Would that not indicate He had greater plans than these which seem so paramount to us? They do not cease from service when they leave our side. These qualities admired by earth are equally attractive to the Master. The hands that were ever busy here are not idle. Their voices do not cease to praise Him. They are serving Him in a wider field, unhampered by human limitations.

If our loved ones are ours forever, we should not go through the trying months in an atmosphere suggesting they are gone; that we have lost them. Much of our thinking about death is as unchristian as our attitude toward life. Let us continue to speak their names and talk of them as naturally as we have always done. How cruel and unkind we are when we try to forget! They do not forget us. They are still faithful. They speak our name. They are as much a part of our life and home as before, and to remain silent is to do them an injustice. Perhaps the first thing we do is remove from our sight that which their hands have touched. Is there a better way of holding their hands in ours than by keeping always within reach those objects that meant the most to them? Do you still read the letters they sent? I have sacredly kept every one, from the first that merely indicated friendship, to the last that reveals a deep concern because I was forced to carry on my ministry alone while she was being prepared in another city for hospitalization. These keepsakes are the only things earthly we have of them, apart from pleasant and happy memories. To allow the flowers to die they so carefully nurtured is to be unfaithful. The unfailing trust they had in us through life must be continued. We cannot destroy it. They still trust

OUT-LIVED SORROW

us and have confidence in our love and loyalty. In truth, our efforts to preserve the best that was theirs will pay us rich dividends, and will increase their happiness. Susie C. Love in her poem, "For You," written after the death of her husband, who was a minister, says,

> The things you loved I have not laid away
>   To molder in the darkness, year by year;
> The songs you sang, the books you read each day
>   Are all about me, intimate and dear.
>
> I do not keep your chair a thing apart,
>   Lonely and empty — desolate to view —
> But if one comes a-weary, sick at heart,
>   I seat him there and comfort him — for you.
>
> I do not go apart in grief and weep,
>   For I have known your tenderness and care;
> Such memories are joy that we may keep,
>   And so I pray for those whose lives are bare.
>
> I may not daily go and scatter flowers
>   Where you are sleeping 'neath the sun and dew —
> But if one lies in pain through weary hours,
>   I send the flowers there, dear heart, for you.
>
> Perchance so much that now seems incomplete
>   Was left for me in my poor way to do.
> And I shall love to tell you — when we meet —
>   That I have done your errands, dear, for you.

In the second place, our sorrow is turned into joy through a growing consciousness of our loved one's nearness. Death does not separate. True, we cannot see their face, but their presence is so keenly felt that continued fellowship with them is as natural as our communion with the Master. There are times when we would not be surprised if the door opened and they walked in upon us as they once did, with the same contagious smile and familiar greeting. "It's a strange thing," said Dinah Morris in *Adam Bede*, "sometimes when I'm quite alone, sitting in my room with my eyes closed, or walking over the hills, the people I've seen and known, if it's only been for a few days, are brought before me, and I hear their voices and see them look and move almost plainer than I ever did when they were really with me so as I could touch them." And it does seem that way to us who fondly keep looking in their direction. We do not see them as clearly as we should when they are with us. They are taken too much for granted, and regardless of our love, the minor flaws blind us to the true proportions of their life. That is why, with Dinah Morris, we see them "plainer" than we did when, buoyant and healthy, they brought cheer and sunshine to our home. The disciples did not see Jesus as He really was until after the resurrection. And He indicated that He must leave them in order to draw closer. "It is expedient for you," He said, "that I go away."

Coupled with their nearness is their understanding. To be near is to know. They are not blind to our stumblings or our brave, steady steps. Neither are they deaf to the words we feebly mumble, or courageously proclaim.

I realize that such an understanding brings with it problems. Will they be always happy knowing so

OUT-LIVED SORROW

much? Would we not cause them pain? Perhaps so, but would their deepest yearnings be any different in Heaven than upon earth? They knew our limitations while here, yet they loved and forgave us. They surely would not want to be denied that privilege now, for their interest in us has not waned. Instead, it has deepened, grown to the point where blindness to the faults of those for whom their hearts yearn would not be conducive to happiness. But why stress our shortcomings, as though our lives would be so sinful that sadness would always be upon their hearts? Our duty as Christians is to live righteously, and if our love is sincere we would do only that which would contribute to their greater happiness.

Their nearness likewise suggests unlimited power. Being no longer confined by human limitations, should they not be able to do more for us? Like the Master they are always with us, and like Him they continue to serve. They who prayed for us here will not cease to speak on our behalf. "If the apostles and martyrs, while still in the body, are able to pray for others — how much more may they do so now? Shall their powers be less after they have begun to be with Christ?" So said Jerome in the fourth century. We tend to think of them as weak and helpless at the precise moment their powers are increased beyond human understanding. How are we to know what proportion of strength and courage coming to us daily is the result of their tender ministry or intercession? We realize that power has been given, and those who love us are not idle. When discouragements come,

LIFE BEGINS WITH JESUS

would they not console us as always? When loneliness settles upon us, are they not by our side? And the work they left, whether in home or church, have they completely withdrawn from that? The desires and aspirations that have led to the betterment of the race cannot be destroyed by death. In a wider and more thorough way it is continued. While still active, Edwin Markham wrote this as his own epitaph:

> Here, now, the dust of Edwin Markham lies.
> But, lo! he is not here; he is afar,
> On life's great errands, under brighter skies.

And today Edwin Markham, one of the world's best loved poets, is "on life's great errands," for the greatest of all began some time ago when his eyes first opened in that Celestial City. The limited vision life affords is past for our loved ones. They see with new eyes and inspire and lead accordingly. Their errands are the most essential as Heaven views them, and how many deal with us and our problems we will know only when all is explained. Of this we are certain, we are not alone. Not only is God with us and the Master our constant companion, but those who had a share with us in life's burdens, add strength and direction to that of the Eternal.

To be near indicates increasing love. Love does not decay, but grows stronger with death. It loses none of its warmth or tenderness. The bonds that held us together cannot and will not be broken. Henry E. Manning has so aptly said, "Shall they love us less because they now are able to love us more." Even here love lingers to the end. As long as conscious-

OUT-LIVED SORROW

ness remains love is the last to leave a life. The body might lose its power and disease be in complete control, with death but hours away, yet love continues unimpaired. Other interests have left the mind, but the last feeble words uttered are expressions of love. Death is powerless to dispose of that. Our dear ones who are so near, continually showering their inexhaustible supply of love upon us, provide the incentive to continue to the end in our fields of service.

To be near one we love is to be ever anxious for their happiness. That is their desire for us. This is always the normal course love takes. Those who wept with us when we wept, would not want us now to weep alone. That would not increase their happiness. Our companion who was so careful to avoid everything destined to bring us pain has not lost that feeling. They note the sorrow that is upon our heart, and if their voice could be heard, the message would be the same consoling one with which we are so familiar. Our unhappiness brings them pain. This does not mean that we are to lightly view our loss. Love cannot do that. Rather does it mean that a knowledge of the joyful surroundings of their new home should bring a corresponding joy to our hearts, together with the realization that their total happiness depends upon the extent of ours.

A dear soul, whose sorrow has been extremely great, related to me this incident: Years before, when she lived in England, death visited the parsonage of their town, taking with it a child upon whom the minister and his wife showered their love. Every night the poor, distraught mother bathed her pillow in tears. One night she had a dream in which she saw a great procession of children in Heaven walking with lighted candles. In the midst of the group was her boy, but his candle was almost extinguished. She called to him, saying, "Tommy, why is your candle so dim and flickering?" Back to her came these words, "I cannot keep my candle lit because your tears continue to put it out." Our loved ones might not have candles in that land of endless day, but perhaps our tears do much to partially extinguish the light of happiness and joy that rightfully belongs to them.

To be near is to be within speaking distance. We soon realize that our conversation is in Heaven as well as upon earth. We understand anew the meaning of Communion of Saints. Much of this might sound irrelevant to the person who has suffered no loss. It is not irrelevant to us who, with a broken heart, enter our home and there for the first time find no loved one with whom we can talk. Our minds naturally turn in their direction and, as of old, we speak as we did in days past. And why not? They are not dead! How foolish to feel that no words again can be spoken until that day when they stand with shining faces to welcome us. We still need their encouragement and counsel. If their interest in us has not changed, should ours for them? And they are anxious to hear from us, these loved ones. Just as anxious as we are to hear from them. "On both sides," said Cyprian to his friend Cornelius, "let us always pray for each other." Yes, and talk over matters

OUT-LIVED SORROW

that always have been of mutual interest. Heaven is not an isolated city, lacking contact with the world. Life is continuous and our own do not want to be deprived of that which was so helpful while on earth. Our sorrow will not turn into joy if we feel that their lips are silent and ours must also remain mute.

If you have dear ones just beyond your human reach, don't be afraid or ashamed to talk with them. You have been given that desire for a purpose. God does not waste His gifts. And they expect it as much as our Master expects us to commune with Him. Don't hesitate to remind them of your love. God understands. He knows that you cannot love them more, who are in His care, without loving Him more, who cares for them. One thing Jesus did was to remove the stiff, unnatural barriers that existed between this life and the next. We do not add anything to our faith, much less our happiness, when we put them back again.

In the third place, our sorrow is turned into joy because we become increasingly aware of God's sympathy and love. I read sometime ago a sermon written by a minister who had survived death after all hope had been abandoned. His story was not only a reminder of the valuable lessons pain had taught, but it was an unfolding revelation of the sympathy, ministry, and love of God. In much the same way as Isaiah in the temple, he caught a new vision of the Eternal unlike that which he had seen during the preceding years of faithful, consecrated service. It reminded me of the first sermons I preached after the devastating flood and hurricane that caught and held us in its vise-like grip. They were different. They had to be. My faith had not changed, but the disaster focused my attention as never before on the goodness of God. And I was not alone in this feeling. Never have I heard the hymns of the church sung with more feeling and fervor, than by the men and women who had left the scene of desolation long enough to assemble for prayer and worship. They lost much, but gained more. And the expression in their tear-dimmed eyes, together with the light upon their soiled faces, spoke of something that cannot be accurately recorded. It is this that comes to the Christian when, for a little while, he bids good-bye to the one who has shared in the problems, difficulties, and joys of his home.

The goodness, love, and sympathy of God enables us to understand that He not only bestows His love upon the one entering His presence, but He is by our side also. We might be uncertain and weak in our affirmation at first, as we dazedly grope our way through the maze of problems that have suddenly arisen, but not for long. We soon realize that He, too, is conscious of our loss, and knows what it means. It is then He draws closer, until we feel beneath us the strength of the everlasting arms. "My God shall supply all your need according to his riches in glory by Christ Jesus," wrote the great Apostle. And He will. We can be sure of that. He who is responsible for Heaven has not only made ample preparation for those who inherit it, but has planned extensively for

OUT-LIVED SORROW

us who remain. Heaven's blessings have no bounds. God adds to our life the instant He bestows so much upon those who are ushered into His presence. How could we continue without this added strength? We might not be able to discern that gift immediately following the committal service for our own. But let us look back, and it will be with astonishment that we did so much. Never once did we falter. Not one responsibility was neglected. We could not do that of ourselves. That is the result of God's guarantee. That is what Horace Bushnell had in mind when he said, "If your life is dark, then walk by faith; and God is pledged to keep you as safe as if you could understand everything." Times such as that are not easy, but He has guaranteed to be with us and see us through. "When thou passest through the waters, I will be with thee," is a promise that remains unbroken.

An artist caught this picture of God many years ago when he painted Christ upon the cross enveloped in darkness. At first glance this would appear to be a gloomy picture of the crucifixion, but on closer inspection is to be seen another form, with sorrow upon His face, lovingly upholding the Master. That is what He does for us. Our sorrow becomes His sorrow, but it doesn't end there. He does more than weep and offer a few encouraging words. He upholds and sustains us by way of His love until the surrounding darkness disappears.

Grief leaves a wound upon our heart in much the same way an injury leaves one upon our body. But grief is not permanent, because God intended otherwise.

LIFE BEGINS WITH JESUS

As the wound on our body heals, so does the wound in our heart. Only the scar remains and scars but indicate that there was once pain. They are always a reminder, and certainly none of us would want to forget. They are an indication that God can heal even the sorest wound. He, however, does more than that. He develops as He heals. It is in sorrow that God makes a man. He not only upholds, He molds a life, making it bigger and stronger. The sad experience against which we bitterly protest does more for us than that for which we fondly reach. We are a novice in the art of development. God holds the secret and time teaches us that it is based upon understanding and love. This is what Ethel M. Milner, in her poem "Be Not Troubled," says.

> Let not your heart be anxious,
>   For things that pass away.
> Expect for each tomorrow,
>   The blessings of today.
> Your faith, it will grow stronger
>   When trials take their toll.
> It takes a crucial testing
>   To make a great man's soul.

And indeed it does! The soul is not developed in any other way. And we who yearn for uninterrupted sunshine ignore the most important ingredient in the making of a successful, well-proportioned life.

When we begin to out-live sorrow we not only realize the sympathetic understanding of God, but we think more of Christ. He consoles us. "I will not leave you comfortless" are His reassuring words. We

OUT-LIVED SORROW

know it to be true, not from hearsay, but through intimate, personal experience. It is in the assurance He gave that we see light and become aware of what He is doing for those we mourn. Our dear ones are in His care. We cannot think of them without a deeper appreciation of Him. He is looking after them, watching over them, satisfying their needs. We did that once, and it is with a sense of joy we behold the skillful hands that now minister. That was His desire while upon earth. "The Son of man came not to be ministered unto, but to minister, and to give his life a ransom for many I am among you as he that serveth." He cannot forget that any more than they can forget to serve and love us. Everything dear to their hearts, becomes dear to ours. To be in His presence brings happiness to them and us. This unites earth and Heaven in a stronger bond. We go forth to build His kingdom with renewed zeal, in deep appreciation of His care over our own.

Let us keep within our hearts the source of life's greatest hope. It will enable us to think more of the Christian faith. That hope is found nowhere else. It is the only power that can turn our sorrow into joy. We will understand the meaning of our grief and know why our faith looms in the dark as it cannot possibly do in the sunshine. It unceasingly reminds us that life begins with Jesus.

www.ingramcontent.com/pod-product-compliance
Lightning Source LLC
Chambersburg PA
CBHW031349040426
42444CB00005B/242